Studies on Entrepreneurship, Structural Change and Industrial Dynamics

The ‘Studies on Entrepreneurship, Structural Change and Industrial Dynamics’ series showcases exceptional scholarly work being developed on the still unexplored complex relationship between entrepreneurship, structural change and industrial dynamics, by addressing structural and technological determinants of the evolutionary pathway of innovative and entrepreneurial activity.

The series invites proposals based on sound research methodologies and approaches to the above topics. Volumes in the series may include research monographs and edited/contributed works.

* * *

This is a SCOPUS-indexed series.

Fabio Greco

Startup Ecosystems

Components for an Interpretative Model and International Benchmarks

Springer

Fabio Greco
Department of Humanities
University of Naples Federico II
Naples, Italy

ISSN 2511-2023 ISSN 2511-2031 (electronic)
Studies on Entrepreneurship, Structural Change and Industrial Dynamics
ISBN 978-3-031-34413-8 ISBN 978-3-031-34414-5 (eBook)
https://doi.org/10.1007/978-3-031-34414-5

This Springer imprint is published by the registered company Springer Nature Switzerland AG
The registered company address is: Gewerbestrasse 11, 6330 Cham, Switzerland

Introduction

Successful startups may enhance a nation's economy by generating new employment possibilities and investment prospects. Startups' ability to succeed is heavily influenced by the environment in which they are placed. In this regard, it is critical to comprehend the startup ecosystem notion from the viewpoint of academics and industry experts.

Evidence suggesting that the most successful startups are centered predominantly in particular regions of the globe led to the need to further explore the ecosystem's dimensions and components and to observe the best ecosystems for startups. This was followed by a comparison with the Italian setting, and this concentration is by no means accidental. In fact, the presence of cities and districts recognized worldwide as real technological hubs appears to be directly connected to the presence of a series of conditions that are extremely favorable to their development.

From this reasoning, the concept of "ecosystem" is defined by us in the course of the work as a "set of conditions, actors and infrastructures capable of supporting the birth and development of innovative business projects; an absolutely heterogeneous system of elements, which embraces culture, regulatory and fiscal measures, public administration, financiers, businesses, universities and research centers."

To better describe the phenomenon of startup ecosystems and analyze the main components that characterize the latter, especially in relation to the geographical contexts in which they develop, we have chosen to start from a model that presents five essential components of startup ecosystems: entrepreneurship with a particular focus on the diffusion of startup companies; business incubators and accelerators; institutions (and in particular universities); and the possibility of accessing technologies as a lever for achieving the main objectives of startups.

A qualitative research approach with many degrees of analysis is presented in the work. The process research is focused on several case studies, where we initially compare the startup ecosystems in Rome and Naples before settling on Silicon Valley as the first standard (despite the constraints it still has today).

The findings of narrative interviews with the key players in the startup ecosystem—founders, incubator and accelerator directors, and university academics interested in the topic of new entrepreneurship—were added to the case studies to enhance them.

Contents

Part II Benchmarking for Start-up Ecosystems

Part I
The Components of the Start-up Ecosystem

A Research Design on Start-up Ecosystems

1 An Overview of Start-up Ecosystems

Start-up businesses are spreading all over the world by exploiting disruptive ideas and recent digital technologies. In 2020, there were approximately 140,000 start-up companies in Europe that created a total of 18,000 jobs. The sectors in which European start-ups are active are mainly IT/software development (19.1%) and software-as-a-service (18.5%). New sectors that are registering more start-ups are Green Technologies (4%) and FinTech (5.1%). An interesting fact is that most start-ups (82.1%) in Europe operate in business-to-business (B2B) markets and generate their turnover entirely (46.5%) or mainly (25.3%) by working with other companies more than with the final market. In the same year, there were 1217 incubators and accelerators for new enterprises, employing 7165 people (Social innovation monitor, 2021). Similar tendencies exist in the United States, although the numbers are far larger. Venture capital investors sank $946 million across 54 deals in the Pacific Northwest during the fourth quarter, according to GeekWire's tally, derived from our running list of Pacific Northwest start-up investments. That follows $1.1 billion raised in the third quarter and a strong first half of 2020 for Seattle and the broader Pacific Northwest start-up ecosystem. Funding totals from 2020 for the region came in at $4.4 billion, up 15% year over year. In Italy, there are now approximately 15,000 businesses registered. Start-up businesses employ over 450,000 people. For 2022, a capital raise of approximately 2 billion euros is predicted (Sole 24 ore, 2022). These metrics imply that the start-up issue not only interests people who aspire to be business owners but is also gaining the interest of practitioners and academics.

Start-ups have characteristics that distinguish them from established businesses; for instance, their growth rate is higher than the industry average. Often, this depends on successful mentorship; indeed, mentored start-ups have quicker growth and a seven-times-higher funding amount than other start-ups. If the statement that start-ups are human institutions designed to create new products and services in

F. Greco, *Startup Ecosystems*, Studies on Entrepreneurship, Structural Change and Industrial Dynamics, https://doi.org/10.1007/978-3-031-34414-5_1

conditions of extreme uncertainty is true (Blank & Dorf, 2013), then it is equally true that these realities are not the small version of traditional businesses. Start-ups require very different rules, paths, skills, and tools. These initiatives bring out a necessary joint effort by a plurality of actors, such as institutions, the state, universities, research centers, venture capitalists, and business incubators (Gibson & Smilor, 1991). Therefore, the entrepreneur, as a central subject in the start-up of new businesses, is no longer alone but flanked by other actors able to facilitate and stimulate the birth of companies in the most varied and innovative forms.

This new complex and dynamic entrepreneurial scenarios in which start-up companies flourish has led scholars to investigate it in more depth in recent years, giving rise to a new study topic that takes the name of "start-up ecosystem."

The entrepreneurial culture that emphasizes innovation is heavily influenced by start-ups. The entrepreneur emerges as the driving force behind progress because he or she enhances society, boosts competition, and boosts output by introducing novel goods and services to the market. Due to their critical role in assisting and directing newly formed economic organizations that lack the resources and capital to successfully navigate their challenging start-up phases, business accelerators, and incubators have received strong support and have positioned themselves as the primary actors in ecosystems. All of this was heavily pushed by the digital revolution and, consequently, by new technologies, which are frequently developed inside start-up organizations. Institutions also play a very significant role, and universities in particular allow for the transfer and interchange of necessary skills.

For the aforementioned reasons, we concentrate on the "start-up ecosystem," which is regarded as a specific economic system in which a group of players works together to build a support system for entrepreneurs by providing them with better and quicker access to services, information, and resources.

2 Impact of COVID-19 and Postpandemic International Scenario: Insight from Global Report Start-Up Genome

The global start-up industry is massive, at roughly $3 trillion. In 2019, approximately $300 billion in venture capital investments were made worldwide. Among the reports consulted and analyzed for the preparation of this book, the author has chosen to refer to global reports on Genome's start-up ecosystems for 2019, 2020, and 2021. Therefore, the rise of new emerging start-up ecosystems around the world has coincided with the explosion of high growth and innovative entrepreneurial initiatives over the past 10 years, which represent the primary growth engine of the economy in several markets. This has an impact on the future of the global economy (Start-up Genome, 2021). Nonetheless, even at the end of 2019, it was not all rainbows and unicorns. The world's major report on the start-up ecosystem of the last 10 years shows that most of the high-growth start-ups, mainly technology-oriented, have emerged from a few start-up ecosystems, such as Silicon Valley and the Boston area. Indeed, value creation by ecosystems remains concentrated, with approximately 74% of all value being concentrated in the top 10 performing cities globally.

Inclusion remains a fundamental challenge for tech ecosystems, with only 14.1% of founders globally being female. The COVID-19 crisis also negatively impacted global start-up ecosystems, as it did all other ecosystems:

- Layoffs are common among start-ups. Start-ups that choose not to lay off employees were forced to cut staff hours through part-time employment.
- Start-ups are facing double pain, i.e., a decline in consumer demand and a decrease in investments in venture capital. Four out of 10 start-ups in the world will die if they do not raise funds as soon as possible because their business costs remain constant and unchanged.

In 2020, the state of the global start-up economy can be seen through two main angles: "*the calm before the storm*," up to December 2019, and the consequences of the COVID-19-triggered crisis.

The latter Start-up' Genome predicted in 2019 that 100 cities would cross the $4 billion threshold in ecosystem value by 2029. It looks like we might hit that milestone even earlier.

Although COVID-19 first had a negative impact on start-ups, by driving digitization, it eventually helped the industry. Tech firms have grown 2.3 times faster than their nontech competitors since the outbreak. The data to emerge are undoubtedly related to the growth of jobs created by start-ups, which have continued to hire despite the persistence of the pandemic crisis. Overall, the emerging data confirm that start-ups continue to create not only employment but also high-profile jobs.

According to Start-up Genome data, just 1.5% of businesses—or approximately 15% of those that survive—produce a successful exit of $50 million or more across the top 8 US start-up ecosystems. The genome study also shows that over 90% of start-ups entirely fail (Fig. 1.1).

The coverage of ecosystems by the start-up genome is growing. Their analysis—which expanded from 60 ecosystems in 2018 to 150 in 2019 and to nearly 300 today—has allowed us to rank the top 40 global start-up ecosystems as well as 100 emerging start-up ecosystems. In the past, our ranking included only the top 30 start-up ecosystems.

To support the purpose of this book, the ecosystems that ranked in the top 10 and the evaluation criteria that Genome used to draw up the ranking are reported.

Finally, we share some key findings of the aforementioned ranking.

The six parameters that the genome report used to classify global ecosystems are as follows: performance, funding, market reach, connectedness, talent, and knowledge.

The top 10 rankings are as follows:

#1 Silicon Valley (North America)
#2 New York City (North America)

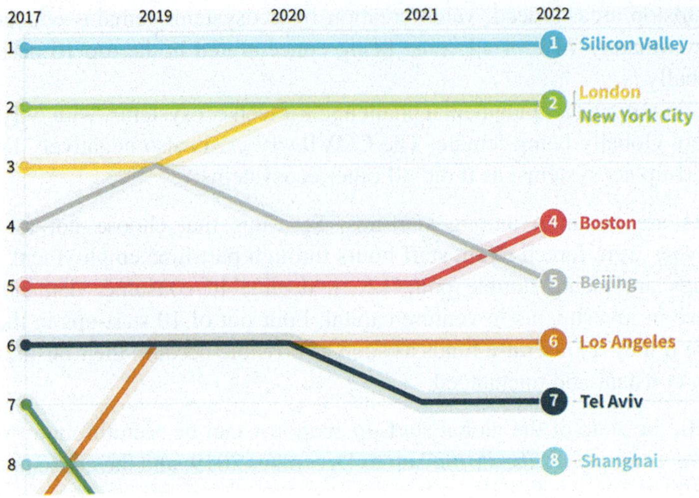

Fig. 1.1 Top 8 start-up ecosystems in the world

#3 London (Europe)
#4 Beijing (Asia Pacific)
#5 Boston (North America)
#6 Tel Aviv—Jerusalem (Europe)
#7 Los Angeles (North America)
#8 Shanghai (Asia Pacific)
#9 Seattle (North America)
#10 Stockholm (Europe).

The key genome ranking findings are as follows:

The top eight global start-up ecosystems remain the same, although with some movement among them compared to previous years.

The 2020 rankings have seen the growth of many R&D powerhouses, i.e., those ecosystems growing largely due to their strengths in research and patent production. Tokyo (#15) and Seoul (#20) are prime examples of this, with both ecosystems scoring the maximum in the Knowledge Factor—a measure of R&D activity. Shenzhen (#22) and Hangzhou (#28) also fit this ecosystem archetype.

The rise of Asia is more visible this year, with 30% of the top ecosystems coming from the region, compared to 20% in 2012. Of the 11 new ecosystems that made it to the top ecosystems list, six are out of the Asia-Pacific.

There are two new entrants in the top 20 global start-up ecosystems: Tokyo (#15) and Seoul (#20). They displace Bangalore (which fell primarily due to low levels of funding) and San Diego.

In addition to Tokyo and Seoul, new entrants among the top 30 include Shenzhen (the advanced manufacturing hub, at #22), Hangzhou (home to Alibaba, at #28), and São Paulo (#30, returning to the top ecosystems list after falling off in 2017).

Six ecosystems debuted in the list of runners-up of top global ecosystems: Salt Lake-Provo and Dallas (tied at #31 with other ecosystems) as well as Copenhagen, Melbourne, Montreal, and Delhi, tied at #36 with Dublin.[1]

3 Main Start-up Ecosystem Conceptualizations

In general, the term "ecosystem" means a biological community of interacting organisms, and their physical environment of interaction is a real system.

The term "ecosystem" was adopted for the first time in the social sciences and economics by Moore (1993), who underlines how the environment external to the company and, therefore, to entrepreneurship—i.e., the "business ecosystem"—is important and affects performance.

Thus, the term "start-up ecosystem" has roots in biology. Defining a start-up ecosystem can also be done somewhat in the same sense. For this reason, most of the management literature defines a start-up ecosystem as an environment made up of people who work there, start-ups in their various phases, and different types of organizations in one place physically or virtually, interacting as a system to create new start-up companies.

To better understand how the studies have gradually converged toward the aforementioned definition, the author believes it is appropriate to review the literature on independent studies that have sought to evaluate what a start-up ecosystem is, bringing to light very different aspects that make the topic very complex. Therefore, through a historical excursus, we will show the genesis of the term adopted in the literature.

Different definitions have spread in the literature, hand in hand with the evolution of the phenomenon, starting from the concepts of ecosystems in economic meaning and the service ecosystem (Lusch & Vargo, 2014; Russo-Spena et al., 2016; Barile & Polese, 2010; Peters et al., 2016) up to talking about very and own start-up ecosystems (Tripathi et al., 2018; Dhakal, 2020; Cukier & Kon, 2018).

In exploring the main contributions throughout the history of studies on business and the environment, and therefore on ecosystems depending on different historical periods, each contribution highlights particular characteristics (Greco & Tregua, 2022).

Starting from the early 1990s, many theoretical contributions have focused on whether the biological comparison with the company is correct for the purposes of describing its development within an interrelated system in which each part has a precise function (Rispoli, 1989; Vicari, 2013; Moore, 1993; Sciarelli, 2004).

Subsequently, after the first decade of the 2000s, many scholars focused on a concept of the environment in which the company operates in a much more complex

[1]Contenuti acquisiti dal report Genome 2022 (startupgenome.com).

manner, defining it as a "business ecosystem" with the importance of very transversal concepts such as those of resources, management of knowledge, corporate culture, and business networks (Moore, 1993; Cohen, 2013; Barney, 2006; Isenberg, 2011). Moore asserts that the ecosystem represents a response to the main challenge of the modern economy, namely, the need to promote innovation and creativity to identify answers to economic and social problems (Moore, 1993).

Immediately after the concept of the ecosystem was once again extended and enriched, the concept of the service ecosystem began to be theorized (Lusch & Vargo, 2014; Mele & Russo-Spena, 2015; Barile & Polese, 2010; Peters et al., 2016). In the context of service ecosystems, the concept of value cocreation view in which service underlies all economic activity according to the service-dominant logic (Lusch & Vargo, 2014). The concept of the start-up ecosystem has formed gradually over time. Although there have been some hints during the past years, we will show that only after 2015 did it experience effective development.

The term "start-up ecosystem" comes from the ground-breaking description of the "business ecosystem" offered by Moore (1993), which characterizes the environment that presents prospects for the launch of new businesses owing to an impressively motivating boost to entrepreneurship (Bala Subrahmanya, 2017). Indeed, empirical investigations also show the positive impact of the activities promoted in start-up ecosystems on both new ventures and the maturation of running firms (Aleisa et al., 2013; Hernández & González, 2016). Additionally, the notion of the start-up ecosystem emerges as a zooming-in on the entrepreneurial ecosystem; Bala Subrahmanya (2017) represents it as the development of contextual opportunities. An inspiring contribution to the tie between entrepreneurs and an ecosystem-based approach has been offered by Lusch and Vargo (2011), who state that a stronger entrepreneurial approach ecosystem can enhance the outcome of resource usage in firms.

A start-up ecosystem is a segment of the broader entrepreneurial ecosystem. The most analyzed connections of the community's entrepreneurial support network are those between entrepreneurs, between formal support organizations, between entrepreneurs and key support entities, and with other organizations (Motoyama & Watkins, 2014). The concept of the start-up ecosystem mirrors the openness to blurring firms' boundaries and favoring the advantages of being part of a broader ecosystem; indeed, an ecosystem is known for its permeability to new stimuli from additional actors, as the dynamics of an ecosystem depend on the openness brought about by its features and tools (Yun et al., 2017). Similarly, a start-up ecosystem as a business context favors the deployment of regional innovation and the expansion of the business environment, with positive outcomes in terms of domestic product and employment (Krajcik & Formanek, 2015). The authors defined the regional start-up ecosystem as an effective method for approving regional innovations and the development of the business environment, as well as ensuring domestic product growth and employment in the country in question. Moreover, a start-up ecosystem is framed as a dynamic context formed by people and start-ups in a system offering chances to create new business ventures (Gobble, 2014).

The following subsections, after an overview of the first and most important conceptualizations, delve into the extant literature on start-up ecosystems from three perspectives, based on actors, geographical contexts, and resources. The three perspectives will then lead to a review of the flourishing literature on incubators and accelerators as support factors for the new era of entrepreneurship.

3.1 Start-Up Ecosystem and the Resources

The first group of contributions the author identifies describes a start-up ecosystem based on the resources shaping it and contributing to its evolution.

There is a definition of "start-up" that emphasizes the importance of the resources that an ecosystem offers or does not offer; indeed, Crowne (2002) describes a start-up as an organization with limited experience, working with inadequate resources, and influenced by several factors, such as investors, customers, competitors, and the use of dynamic product technologies. Great importance is assigned to knowledge and risk capital as resources supporting the setup of a start-up ecosystem and the start-ups and affecting the change to be successful (Hemmert et al., 2016). Furthermore, Malecki (2018) affirms that the nature of an ecosystem is that of an umbrella—as both term and context—and, therefore, an ecosystem is a setting consisting of resources and performing activities because of them. Similarly, Buchnik et al. (2018) state that the performance of a start-up ecosystem depends on the various resources available; they refer to both those usually related to all businesses (such as resources, knowledge, and skills) and those specifically related to new ventures (such as contests, simulations, a learning program made of lectures, courses, and mentoring). Finally, the new approaches toward resource integration and mutual exchange represent stimuli for entrepreneurs, as they give fluidity to start-up ecosystems, favoring the permeability of new competencies, additional actors, and new ways of doing things. These elements are all needed in an innovation-oriented context (Fraiberg, 2017; Quero & Ventura, 2019), but further research has been called for to depict how the activities of start-up communities can be improved and how accelerators' members can impact start-up ecosystems (Cohen, 2019).

Tripathi et al. (2018) explore various definitions of the term "start-up ecosystem" and conclude that a start-up ecosystem involves different stakeholders and support organizations, collaborating in the environment of a particular region to form new start-ups and give impetus to existing ones (Tripathi et al., 2018).

The ecosystem plays a crucial role in these businesses' growth, operation, and reach in addition to ensuring their survival as start-ups. In this age of globalization, appealing to both local and international consumers aids a company's expansion, while overseas investors frequently assess both the business and the environment in which it works (Dhakal, 2020).

It is helpful to include certain nonscientific contributions that are still extremely valuable and relevant in addition to processes with a The OECD provides a definition of "entrepreneurial ecosystem," which acts to be summarized with respect to the main results of previous academic contributions. It refers to the "entrepreneurial ecosystem" as a *set of interconnected potential and existing entrepreneurs, entrepreneurial organizations* (e.g., firms, venture capitalists, business angels, and banks), *institutions* (e.g., universities, public sector agencies, and financial organizations), and *entrepreneurial processes* (e.g., business birth rate, number of start-ups, levels of entrepreneurial ambition, and business failure rate), which *connect and manage performance within the specific entrepreneurial environment, both formally and informally* (Mason & Brown, 2014). Experts' and scholars' focus is increasingly on the "system," considering the market, policy, and culture domains as characterizing elements of an entrepreneurial ecosystem.

Similarly, Start-up Commons states that a start-up ecosystem is an interactive system made up of people, start-ups, and different organizations in a physical or virtual location to facilitate new start-up companies.

3.2 The Importance of Geographic Variables

Some academics who have developed theories regarding start-up ecosystems place much emphasis on geographic factors. One of the contributions adopting such an approach is Cukier and Kon (2018), who define a start-up ecosystem as follows: "a limited region within 30 miles (or one-hour travel) range, formed by people, their start-ups, and various types of supporting organizations, interacting as a complex system to create new start-up companies and evolve the existing ones." Similarly, Cohen starts from the conceptualization of entrepreneurial ecosystem to propose his view of the start-up ecosystem; to do that, he claims that entrepreneurial ecosystems "represent a diverse set of interdependent actors within a geographic region that influence the formation and eventual trajectory of the entire group of actors and potentially the economy. Entrepreneurial ecosystems evolve through a set of interdependent components which interact to generate new venture creation over time" (pp. 2–3). Some years later, Williamson et al. (2013) focused on the social and cultural context as factors supporting innovation and personal characteristics; as a result, due to the inner nature of start-ups, with innovation and the personality of the entrepreneur at their core, the authors describe the start-up ecosystems evolving over time because of the outcomes of innovation and the personal features of the entrepreneurs, primarily from the local context. Audretsch and Belitski suggest a more focused strategy as a result of the attention they gave to cities; thus, the socioeconomic, institutional, and information environment of a city shapes the start-up ecosystem and the start-ups themselves. Similarly, Miles and Morrison (2020) enforce this idea by observing rural contexts; they consider the context as embedded in both the processes leading to the creation of a start-up and the activities they perform.

Cukier and Kon (2018) define a start-up ecosystem as "a limited region within a 30-mile radius (or an hour of travel), made up of people, their start-ups, and various types of support organizations, interacting as a complex system to create new start-ups and make existing ones evolve." The sustainability of the start-up itself depends on the creation of a healthy start-up environment. These start-ups are unlikely to be able to compete with more established companies in their target markets since they have limited financial and intellectual resources.

Ecosystems explain why so many successful start-ups originated in academically and economically strong areas such as Silicon Valley and Singapore. Start-ups have a high failure rate due to their instability, which tends to drop as they interact with ecosystems. Additionally, start-up ecosystems have a substantial economic impact since they boost internal product development and generate new employment that is ensured by the internal flow of ideas, expertise, skills, and resources (Singh et al., 2019).

Among the most recent works on start-up ecosystems anchored to geographical variables, Feld (2020) describes how a start-up ecosystem is shaped in a community and the fundamental principles of a vibrant start-up community. The book examines the attributes of leadership in a start-up community that can help it thrive along with the classic problems any community will face during development. Light is also shed on the territorial institutions of certain communities. These contributions remain very anchored to a territorial dimension. Through this monograph, in reverse, the author hopes for multidimensionality of the phenomenon to overcome this limit.

3.3 The Influence of Market Actors

Finally, the scientific contributions that focus on the concept of start-up ecosystem actors are naturally the most avant-garde ones because they consider an integral and determining part of the start-up ecosystem, not only the start-ups themselves and the end market, not only the start-ups and organizations supporting the latter but all parts of a social context that act to make this ecosystem more vital and flourishing (Mele & Russo-Spena, 2019). According to several authors, start-up ecosystems place much emphasis on actors: Krajcik and Formanek (2015) describe the key role of actors in depicting a start-up ecosystem and its potentialities, stating that (a) actors such as start-ups, policy agencies, incubators, accelerators, and risk capital providers are structural components and (b) openness may favor the joining of new actors because it "is rare to have a complete start-up ecosystem" (p. 15). In a similar vein, Franco-Leal et al. (2019) identify various stages of a start-up ecosystem and state that each of these stages has its tasks and resources; therefore, relationships with actors are necessary to fill the gaps related to both activities to be performed and resources to be integrated.

Laužikas et al. (2015) offer a slightly different view, although still based on actors. In fact, they believe that efforts from both internal and external groups, such as those that promote the growth of new businesses, define the start-up ecosystem. Similarly, Sipola et al. (2016) frame this ecosystem as a setting whose features include contextual factors, a temporal dimension, and renewal mechanisms. The most important contextual determinants are local players and commercial acumen;

preceding economic history and policies, as well as the freshness of start-ups, delineate the temporal dimension; institutions, their dynamism, and the role of failure, on the other hand, contribute to renewal mechanisms. This latter is not considered in the more established literature, as stated by authors borrowing conceptualization from other colleagues. This occurs in the contribution by Cukier and Kon (2018), leaning on Isenberg (2011) to identify regulations, market, finance, knowledge, entrepreneurial capabilities, and entrepreneurship culture as factors affecting the performance of an entrepreneurial ecosystem. Therefore, institutional dynamism in incubators and accelerators favors either the emergence or maturity of start-ups (Joshi & Satyanarayana, 2014).

Incubators and accelerators are critical agents in a start-up ecosystem and the broader entrepreneurship community (Hernández & González, 2016), whose growth is also based on out-of-the-ordinary events, such as TechMeet-up, Open Coffee Club, and Start-up Weekend (Hernández & González, 2016; Paço et al., 2016; Fraiberg, 2017). The entrepreneurship community can be seen as an ecosystem, as in Lusch and Vargo (2011)—namely, "a relatively self-contained, self-adjusting system of resource integrating actors connected by shared institutional logics and mutual value creation through service exchange" (p. 176). Such a view provides evidence of the critical role played by multiple actors, resource integration contexts, an institutional approach representing the working mechanisms of an ecosystem, and the orientation to create value through a service-for-service exchange. Last but not least, researchers studying start-up ecosystems have supported this viewpoint by describing universities and university-based accelerators as components of this ecosystem and its mechanics. (Mansoori et al., 2019). More specifically, they compare universities' roles as elements of the entrepreneurial ecosystem—as in McAdam et al. (2016)—with the role that university-based accelerators play in promoting the growth of start-ups and the formation of new ventures. It is in the field of study with a broader perspective that it is possible to identify the university as an innomediary (Mele & Russo-Spena, 2019) within the start-up ecosystem.

The possibility for universities to become actors in the economic development of a country through the offer of educational-training activities and technology transfer and through the provision of services to start-up companies has in recent years grown the interest of many scholars who have concentrated their research on the relationship between these institutions and new entrepreneurship (Clarysse et al., 2005; Petretto, 2007; Fetters et al., 2010).

Universities have long played a significant role in the development of entrepreneurship in the United States, concentrating their efforts on the management of intellectual property and encouraging the launch of new enterprises both directly and indirectly through the use of university incubators. For instance, more than any other school, Stanford University has been credited with being the catalyst for the emergence and growth of California's high-tech industry. Before the last 10 years, approximately 3000 businesses had been formed by professors, researchers, and students at Stratford University. Stratford University's technological prototypes were instrumental in the founding of businesses such as Sun Microsystem, Cisco

Systems, HP (Hewlett Packard), and Google (Confindustria and Bank of Boston, 2009).

Although slowly, a process of evolution in this direction is also beginning in Europe, where some academic institutions are making significant efforts to support the creation of a more competitive territorial entrepreneurial reality in the face of the perceived lack of collaboration between the academic and business worlds.

4 The Gaps of the Studies and the Purpose of the Book

After reviewing the literature on ecosystems of start-up companies and in relation to the purposes of this work, it is possible to arrive at a first definition that considers most of the main contributions collected and analyzed. *A start-up ecosystem is a set of both potential and existing interconnected factors: entrepreneurial organizations and institutions such as firms, business incubators and accelerators, universities, public sector agencies, venture capitalists, business angels, banks, and start-ups with particularly disruptive and driving ideas and technologies.*

The preliminary study on start-up ecosystems prior to the drafting of this book allowed us to identify some gaps in the studies that preceded us.

The first gap concerns the fact that even the most recent studies discount the fact that for many years, the reference literature has considered the phenomenon of the birth of new innovative businesses as a simple and small component in the broader sphere and phenomenon of entrepreneurship, thus underestimating the topic of start-up ecosystems and causing the absence of a real identity and theoretical connotation for studies on ecosystems of start-up companies.

The second gap concerns scholars' underestimation of the theme of start-up ecosystems, associating it too often with that of innovation ecosystems. In this way, the most important difference between the two types of ecosystems mentioned above—namely, "entrepreneurship"—has been neglected. In fact, both ecosystems present the content of technology and innovation, but innovative ecosystems are not necessarily linked to the variables and dimensions of entrepreneurship as much as start-up ecosystems are. A third gap was analyzed: The literature of the past has often treated start-up ecosystems in the same way as the phenomenon of business incubators and accelerators. However, through this study, we discover that start-up ecosystems are very complex and articulated ecosystems of which business incubators, while of strategic importance, are only a single part. Finally, another lack revealed by the study of the relevant literature is the absence of real managerial implications on the subject. Cohen (2013) has identified how accelerators help start-ups perform better and has identified in which phase of the life cycle these are most essential. Cohen (2019) has even studied the design of the incubation and acceleration process but has limited herself to focusing on support organizations and not on all actors of start-up ecosystems. Similarly, Guerrero et al. (2020) conducted a study on entrepreneurial–university ecosystems evaluating whether university careers would facilitate entrepreneurial success. However, the study is limited to entrepreneurial ecosystems in general without a specific focus on the start-up segment.

The gap analysis makes it clear that the literature prior to these studies certainly focused on the description of start-up ecosystems as an emerging phenomenon but paid little attention to identifying the specific components, actors, and processes that, through very complex dynamics, influence the entrepreneurial ecosystems, determining the well-being of the start-ups located within them.

This has led to the lack of a theoretical framework for start-up ecosystems and, consequently, the lack of managerial implications.

The research aims to provide an interpretative model of start-up business ecosystems by analyzing the main components of the latter and describing any determinants of these types of ecosystems that can favor or disadvantage the development of new innovative ventures. The research question aims to understand how they support the development of start-ups and, parallel to this, how they contribute to the viability of the start-up companies that are part of it and the variables of start-up ecosystems that have a major impact in some contexts about influencing the well-being and development of start-ups. Additionally, can the influence, weight, and importance of these identified variables and components vary depending on the geographical contexts in which the start-up ecosystems are located?

We investigate the different features, origins, and ways of operating the actors who are part of the start-up ecosystems and how these components can impact the birth and development of start-ups. The best practices of some start-up ecosystems in certain areas of the world together with the particular dynamics of other parts of the world will be described. We will explore both excellent, famous start-up ecosystems and lower-performing and less-known international start-up ecosystems.

Two cases of Italian start-up ecosystems (Rome and Naples) will be studied to describe and identify variables that could be defined as important conditions for the birth and development of start-ups, with particular attention given to the role of universities and, therefore, of start-up incubators.

We analyze the starting point and current state of the Italian start-up ecosystem "spliced" into two microecosystems (Rome and Naples), which, although belonging to a similar sociocultural context, have very different operation models. Then, we proceed to a short benchmark with the most famous and productive innovation cluster in the world, namely, that of Silicon Valley, observing the main features, processes, and methods through which networks of highly performing actors are created.

The choice of these ecosystems was made to obtain a heterogeneous sample in terms of size, output, life stage, mode of birth, and "prestige." (Remember that Naples and Rome are not even mentioned in the first report in the world on start-up ecosystems, while San Francisco still ranks first.)

The case studies will also highlight whether the presence of common factors exists despite sociocultural and geographical diversity, providing results that, even if partial, provide some input for future research on start-up ecosystems.

Studying these different scenarios and attempting to answer this research question can also contribute to other research questions and, therefore, the work of other researchers, such as works that focus on the factors that determine or somehow influence the success, failure, and, more generally, development of start-ups.

5 Research Methodology

The methodology of the book adopted a qualitative approach (Dubois & Gadde, 2002) due to the nature of the topic being basically related to the features and components of the start-up ecosystem and the novelty of the debate. Choice is in line with previous studies in entrepreneurship, such as Goyal et al. (2016), opting for a two-step analysis to first frame the context and then analyze it in detail. Indeed, an initial screening of start-up ecosystems was performed to frame the scenario and acquire general knowledge of their activities; the evidence of these ecosystems was combined with the key themes arising from the literature to outline our research process. More specifically, broadness is recommended in the initial phase(s) of research to avoid discarding relevant elements and to obtain an overall perspective on the problem under investigation (Yin, 2009). Such a posture proved to be useful for research carried out with open interviews. Thus, the author investigated the key themes in the wider context of the most relevant start-up ecosystems, three start-up ecosystems, aiming to acquire practical insights into the activities they performed.

Three start-up ecosystems that are very different from each other were chosen. The first two are Italian ecosystems with opposite functioning models but inserted in a similar economic and cultural context. The third, probably the most important in the world, that of Silicon Valley, was chosen because it operates in a practically opposite cultural economic scenario. The first two chosen start-up ecosystems are not even mentioned in the main global report on international start-up ecosystems (Report Genome), while the third ranks first in the same report.

5.1 Research Process

Regarding the first step, the findings started with a desk analysis of the Start-up Ecosystem Report issued by Genome; through the report, the author established an exploratory research process, as in Hernández and González (2016) in dealing with the same topic and in Goyal et al. (2016) aimed at scanning the main topics dealing with a population of business entities, as UBAs are in this case.

As a second step, three cases were chosen to start data collection and set our case study protocol (Yin, 2009) to draw systematically from the knowledge acquired in the first step of analysis and to infuse contextual evidence, as also suggested by Stake (1995). Therefore, the second step was based on the investigation of topics derived from both the literature review and the first step of analysis. In this second step, the method we used was convenience sampling (e.g., Oppong, 2013), as we had to consider the need for in-depth information and the opportunity to obtain direct insights from and interviews with well-informed members of these contexts. Moreover, interviews on entrepreneurship from an ecosystem-based perspective have already been chosen by other scholars (e.g., Spigel, 2017).

The three start-up ecosystems with an embedded UBA chosen for this analysis were NAPLES—Campania New Steel (hereinafter CNS) and ROME—Luiss EnLabs (hereinafter LEL). Additionally, these two contexts offer the advantage of obtaining information from two different approaches because only one of the accelerators participates in the funding of start-ups. The third ecosystem is Silicon Valley in San Francisco does not have a business accelerator acting as a centralized catalyst, but as we shall see, it works differently. Also interviewed representatives of the institutions that participated in shaping start-up ecosystems. In particular, we chose, within the partner universities of the accelerators, the professors who deal with entrepreneurship to bring entrepreneurship as close as possible to university teaching and to activate as many collaborations as possible between these two components.

For the interviews with the actors of the ecosystems of Rome and San Francisco, a narrative analysis approach was adopted. Narrative analysis is an approach to the elicitation and analysis of language that is sensitive to the sense of temporal sequence that people, as tellers of stories about their lives or events around them, detect in their lives and surrounding episodes and inject into their accounts.

Inroads have been made into business and management research in the last 20 years (Czarniawska, 1997; Boje, 2001). The narrative approach was ideal for this book because it allowed us to receive information on key dynamics of the changes in organizations and actors and the relationships between them.

An emblematic example using a narrative approach in a way similar to ours is that of Boje (1991), who analyzed the types and uses of stories in an office supply firm based on his participant observation in the organization and interviews with key actors.

For the interviews with the Campania new steel incubator in Naples and the staff of the Federico II University of Naples, we did not limit ourselves to the narrative approach but also used a phenomenological approach. In fact, the author is an integral part of the latter ecosystem as an Assistant professor at Federico II of Naples and founder of a food delivery premium start-up (Academic Spin-off) that has undertaken the acceleration path of the certified incubator and partner of the aforementioned "Campania New Steel."

We believe the phenomenological approach is important as an integration of the narrative approach because the contribution of the author as a leading actor in the investigation corresponds to the question of how individuals make sense of the world around them and how an individual (the author, in this case) interprets the reality surrounding him.

An emblematic example in the literature is "interpretivism in action" (Grint, 2000), which uses the example of Richard Branson to show how Branson instilled an ideological commitment to a goal by building a vision in which fun rather than rewards is seen as a reason to be associated with the Virgin brand and how Branson also created an image of himself as an entrepreneur intent on protecting the interests of the consumer.

References

Aleisa, E., Recker, J., Liddle, R., & Brown, T. (2013). *Start-up ecosystems. Study of the ecosystems around the world* (pp. 1–38). Focusing on Silicon Valley.

Bala Subrahmanya, M. H. (2017). How did Bangalore emerge as a global hub of tech start-ups in India? Entrepreneurial ecosystem—Evolution, structure and role. *Journal of Developmental Entrepreneurship, 22, 1750006*.

Barile, S., & Polese, F. (2010). Smart service systems and viable service systems: Applying system theory to service science. *Service Science, 2*(1–2), 21–40.

Barney, J. B. (2006). Risorse, competenze e vantaggi competitivi: manuale di strategia aziendale.

Blank, S., & Dorf, B. (2013). *Startupper: Guida alla creazione di imprese innovative*. EGEA spa.

Boje, D. M. (1991). Consulting and change in the storytelling organisation. *Journal of Organizational Change Management, 4*(3), 7–17.

Boje, D. (2001). *Narrative methods for organizational & communication research* (pp. 1–160). Saga.

Buchnik, T., Gilad, V., & Maital, S. (2018). Universities' influence on student decisions to become entrepreneurs: Theory and evidence. *Journal of Entrepreneurship Education, 21*(3), 1–19.

Cohen, S. L. (2013). *How to accelerate learning: Entrepreneurial ventures participating in accelerator programs* (Doctoral dissertation, The University of North Carolina at Chapel Hill), 2013, 14803.

Cohen, S. (2019). What do accelerators do? Insights from incubators and angels. In *Innovation technology, governance, globalization* (Vol. 8, p. 8).

Clarysse, B., Wright, M., Lockett, A., Van de Velde, E., & Vohora, A. (2005). Spinning out new ventures: A typology of incubation strategies from European research institutions. *Journal of Business Venturing, 20*(2), 183–216.

Crowne, M. (2002, August). Why software product start-ups fail and what to do about it. Evolution of software product development in start-up companies. In *IEEE international Engineering Management Conference* (Vol. 1, pp. 338–343). IEEE.

Cukier, D., & Kon, F. (2018). A maturity model for software start-up ecosystems. *Journal of Innovation and Entrepreneurship, 7*(1), 14.

Czarniawska, B. (Ed.). (1997). *A narrative approach to organization studies*. Sage Publications.

Dhakal, M. (2020). *Creating a functioning start-up ecosystem: Case study Finland.*

Dubois, A., & Gadde, L. E. (2002). Systematic combining: An abductive approach to case research. *Journal of Business Research, 55*, 553–560.

Feld, B. (2020). *Start-up communities: Building an entrepreneurial ecosystem in your city*. John Wiley & Sons.

Fetters, M., Patricia, G., & Rice, M. P. (2010). *The development of university-based entrepreneurship ecosystems*. Global Practices.

Fraiberg, S. (2017). Start-up nation: Studying transnational entrepreneurial practices in Israel's start-up ecosystem. *Journal of Business and Technical Communication, 31*(3), 350–388.

Franco-Leal, N., Camelo-Ordaz, C., Fernandez-Alles, M., & Sousa-Ginel, E. (2019). The entrepreneurial ecosystem: Actors and performance in different stages of evolution of academic spinoffs. *Entrepreneurship Research Journal, 10*(2).

Gibson, D. V., & Smilor, R. W. (1991). Key variables in technology transfer: A field-study based empirical analysis. *Journal of Engineering and Technology Management, 8*(3–4), 287–312.

Goyal, S., et al. (2016). *Understanding the challenges and strategic actions of social entrepreneurship at base of the pyramid* (Vol. 54, p. 418). Emerald Onsight.

Greco, F., & Tregua, M. (2022). It gives you wheels: The university-based accelerators in start-up ecosystems. *International Journal of Entrepreneurship and Small Business, 45*(2), 235–257.
Grint, K. (2000). *The arts of leadership*. OUP Oxford.
Gobble, M. M. (2014). Charting the innovation ecosystem. *Research-Technology Management, 57*(4), 55–59.
Guerrero, M., Urbano, D., & Gajón, E. (2020). Entrepreneurial university ecosystems and graduates' career patterns: Do entrepreneurship education programmes and university business incubators matter? *Journal of Management Development, 39*(5), 753–775.
Hemmert, M., Cheng, Y., Kohlbacher, F., Kotosaka, M., Loh, C. T., & Waldenberger, F. (2016). *High-tech start-up ecosystems in east Asian agglomerations: Are they different from the west* (pp. 1–39). German Institute of Japanese Studies.
Hernández, C., & González, D. (2016). Study of the start-up ecosystem in Lima, Peru: Collective case study. *Latin American Business Review, 17*(2), 115–137.
Isenberg, D. (2011). How to foment an entrepreneurial revolution. *The Babsos Entrepreneurship Ecosystem Project, 781*(7).
Joshi, K., & Satyanarayana, K. (2014). What ecosystem factors impact the growth of high-tech start-ups in India? *Asian Journal of Innovation and Policy, 3*(2), 216–244.
Krajcik, V., & Formanek, I. (2015). Regional start-up ecosystem. *European Business & Management, 1*(2), 14–18.
Laužikas, M., Tindale, H., Bilota, A., & Bielousovaitė, D. (2015). Contributions of sustainable start-up ecosystem to dynamics of start-up companies: The case of Lithuania. *Entrepreneurship and Sustainability Issues, 3*, 8–24.
Lusch, R. F., & Vargo, S. L. (2011). Service-dominant logic: A necessary step. *European Journal of Marketing, 45*(7/8), 1298–1309.
Lusch, R. F., & Vargo, S. L. (2014). *The service-dominant logic of marketing: Dialogue, debate, and directions*. Routledge.
Malecki, E. J. (2018). Entrepreneurship and entrepreneurial ecosystems. *Geography Compass, 12*(3), e12359.
Mele, C., & Russo-Spena, T. (2015). Innomediary agency and practices in shaping market innovation. *Industrial Marketing Management, 44*, 42–53.
Mele, C., & Russo-Spena, T. (2019). Innovation in sociomaterial practices: The case of IoE in the healthcare ecosystem. In *Handbook of service science, Volume II* (pp. 517–544). Springer.
Mansoori, Y., Karlsson, T., & Lundqvist, M. (2019). The influence of the lean start-up methodology on entrepreneur-coach relationships in the context of a start-up accelerator. *Technovation, 84*, 37–47.
Mason, C., & Brown, R. (2014). *Entrepreneurial ecosystems and growth oriented entrepreneurship* (Vol. 30, No. 1, pp. 77–102). Final report to OECD, Paris.
McAdam, M., Miller, K., & McAdam, R. (2016). Situated regional university incubation: A multilevel stakeholder perspective. *Technovation, 50*, 69–78.
Miles, M. P., & Morrison, M. (2020). An effectual leadership perspective for developing rural entrepreneurial ecosystems. *Small Business Economics, 54*, 933–949.
Moore, J. F. (1993). Predators and prey. *Harvard Business Review, 71*, 75–86.
Motoyama, Y., & Watkins, K. (2014). Examining the connections within the start up ecosystem. *Kauffman Research Series on City, Metro, and Regional Entrepreneurship.*
Oppong, S. H. (2013). The problem of sampling in qualitative research. *Asian Journal of Management Sciences and Education, 2*(2), 202–210.
Paço, A., Ferreira, J., & Raposo, M. (2016). Development of entrepreneurship education programmes for HEI students: The lean start-up approach. *Journal of Entrepreneurship Education, 19*(2), 39.
Petretto, L. (2007). *Imprenditore ed Università nello start up di impresa, ruoli e relazioni critiche*. Firenze University Press.
Russo-Spena, T., Mele, C., & Nuutinen, M. (Eds.). (2016). *Innovating in practice: Perspectives and experiences*. Springer.

Peters, L. D., Taillard, M., Pels, J., & Mele, C. (2016). The role of shared intentions in the emergence of service ecosystems. *Journal of Business Research, 69*(8), 2972–2980.

Quero, M. J., & Ventura, R. (2019). Value proposition as a framework for value cocreation in crowdfunding ecosystems. *Marketing Theory, 19*(1), 47–63.

Rispoli, M. (Ed.). (1989). *L'impresa industriale: economia, tecnologia, management.* Il mulino.

Sciarelli, S. (2004). Fondamenti di economia e gestione delle imprese. *Cedam.*

Singh, S., Sinha, S., Das, V. M., & Sharma, A. (2019). A framework for linking entrepreneurial ecosystem with institutional factors: A modified total interpretive structural modelling approach. *Journal for Global Business Advancement, 12*(3), 382–404.

Sipola, S., Puhakka, V., & Mainela, T. (2016). A start-up ecosystem as a structure and context for high growth. In *Global entrepreneurship: Past, present & future* (pp. 179–202). Emerald Group Publishing Limited.

Spigel, B. (2017). The relational organization of entrepreneurial ecosystems. *Entrepreneurship Theory and Practice, 41*(1), 49–72.

Stake, R. E. (1995). *The art of case study research.* Sage.

Tripathi, V., Singh, A. P., & Roy, R. (2018). Effect of economic growth initiatives on regional economies: A study in the Indian context. *International Journal of Entrepreneurship and Innovation Management, 22*(3), 286–297.

Vicari, S. (2013). All of us have a problem: rilevanza e rigore nelle discipline manageriali. *Economia & Management, 2013*(3), 1–10.

Williamson, J. M., Lounsbury, J. W., & Han, L. D. (2013). Key personality traits of engineers for innovation and technology development. *Journal of Engineering and Technology Management, 30*(2), 157–168.

Yin, R. K. (2009). *Case study research: Design and methods* (4th ed.). Sage.

Yun, J. J., Won, D., Park, K., Yang, J., & Zhao, X. (2017). Growth of a platform business model as an entrepreneurial ecosystem and its effects on regional development. *European Planning Studies, 25*(5), 805–826.

Studies on Entrepreneurship and the Phenomenon of Start-Ups

1 Introduction

In this chapter, we take as a reference the main contributions in the field of entrepreneurs and entrepreneurship, and we propose to "photograph" a state of the art of studies of these two concepts from the very beginning, subsequently comparing them with the studies on new entrepreneurship in reference to the diffusion of start-up companies. The development of the terms "entrepreneur" and "entrepreneurship" over time is crucial to note, as many academics have described it as "disordered" and "asymmetrical" (Hirsch, 2011; Bygrave, 2006). To explore new forms of innovative entrepreneurship, ways to make them as prosperous as possible and to observe and research the factors that affect the success or failure of these new forms of entrepreneurial enterprises known as start-up companies, it seems essential to first clarify how the figure of the entrepreneur has been interpreted by the scientific literature in the past. Given the volume of contributions on the subject of entrepreneurship, the objective is highly challenging but necessary if we want to understand the situation and promote research.

2 The Entrepreneur in the Management Literature

It is considered useful that the major worldwide scientific publications will be critically reread in the paragraph that follows.

The theoretical framework of Matricano (2015) served as our starting point to present a literature evaluation on entrepreneurship that was as comprehensive as feasible. For industry researchers to suggest the following developments, entrepreneurship studies must have their own theoretical paradigm, much like studies in other disciplines. This is particularly challenging in the case of entrepreneurship since the latter is impacted by other sciences that, while adding to its complexity,

F. Greco, *Startup Ecosystems*, Studies on Entrepreneurship, Structural Change and Industrial Dynamics, https://doi.org/10.1007/978-3-031-34414-5_2

also enhance it. Therefore, it is impossible to use a single interpretative paradigm, but there is a need to use "a multidimensional investigation approach" (Matricano, 2015, p. 30). Attempts to construct entrepreneurial ideas are greatly influenced by interdisciplinarity. So much so that some academics (Kuratko & Audretsch, 2009; Wiklund et al., 2011) contend that to properly balance diverse schools of thought for their research, they must recognize the complexity of entrepreneurial phenomena. It seems obvious and almost unnecessary to stress again that such methods should not advocate investigating the phenomenon of entrepreneurship in a piecemeal fashion by examining different occurrences in isolation but rather that they should be viewed as a whole.

The purpose of a multidisciplinary study is precisely to find the right balance and the right relationship between the different disciplines.

By keeping in mind some guiding principles supported by the literature, such as those of "proximity" and "compatibility," the ideal relationship can be attained. Okhuysen and Bonardi (2011) define "compatibility" as "the extent to which theories that are brought together rely on similar or dissimilar individual decision-making processes, organizational mechanisms, or other properties in the development of their explanations," and "proximity" as "the conceptual distance that exists between the phenomena that the lenses address in their original conception" (Okhuysen & Bonardi, 2011, p. 7).

The ideas of "sensemaking" and "sensegiving," which can help strike the correct balance between multidisciplinary methods, are further ideas (Corley & Gioia, 2011). Through these initiatives, we hope to focus upcoming research on issues that, as the nexus of theory and practice, enable the emergence of fresh lines of inquiry.

2.1 The Four Approaches for a Multidimensional Study of Entrepreneurship

To gather the initial conceptualizations of the entrepreneur, we have chosen a theoretical framework based on four methods.

As a result, the reading above employs four key approaches: a historical approach (Marx, 1964; Weber, 1904), a functional method (Timmons et al., 2004; Hirsch, 2011), a psychological approach (Kirzner, 1973; Ciappei et al., 2006), and a Multivocal Strategic approach (MacMillan & Katz, 1992; Venkataraman & Sarasvathy, 2005; Matricano, 2015) which, in the end, consider an overview of these traditional approaches while integrating them with the new concepts of environment, networks, and open innovation to create an approach that, in fact, had its roots in some classical studies but developed in more recent studies of entrepreneurship, contributing to an analysis of new innovative entrepreneurship (Drucker, 1985; Chesbrough, 2003; Sarasvathy et al., 2008; Blank, 2017) at the basis of the phenomenon of the spread and proliferation of start-ups.

2.1.1 Historical Approach

The historical approach (Marx, 1964; Weber, 1904; Parsons & Smelser, 1956) encompasses the different theoretical frameworks of the concept of entrepreneur mainly in reference to the historical phases and the reasons in terms of historical social variables that explain the spread and genesis of the phenomenon. The historical approach encompasses the differences. This approach is therefore based on the identification of specific sociocultural variables in certain historical periods that have favored the spread of entrepreneurial activity and the configuration of specific types of entrepreneurs. Most of the theoretical contributions of this approach come from social historians of capitalism. According to these authors, the configurations of the various types of entrepreneurs are certainly based on the motivations of the subjects but are in any case influenced by the ideological and social variables of each historical period.

For example, in the studies of Karl Marx, the entrepreneur is identified as one who is possessed by the lust for wealth because driven by a capitalist society that is only a stage in the historical development of humanity (Marx, 1964).

Contrary to the studies of MArx but always with a view to a historical social framework, there are those of Max Weber. According to this scholar, the entrepreneur's vocation and his role are something "transcendental" almost of a religious nature. The vocation and activity of the entrepreneur in the era of capitalism, according to Weber, correspond to "economic rationalism." Through the latter, the individualistic and competitive will of the entrepreneur in Marx's vision is overcome, but on the contrary, it is argued that the modern entrepreneur (of that era) produces for the common good because God wants it (Weber, 1904).

2.1.2 Functional Approach

The functional approach (Cantillon, 1755; Smith, 1776; Knight, 1921) contains theoretical contributions on the entrepreneur that specifically emphasize the concept of business function and purpose. As a result, these theoretical contributions define the various meanings of entrepreneur figures based on the functions they carry out, identifying the entrepreneurial phenomenon in the performance of specific functions or in the possession of specific requirements. Therefore, this strategy places special emphasis on the components that make up the essential components of the function of the entrepreneur. The emblem of this approach is undoubtedly the contribution of Cantillon, where precise content and particular functional relevance are given for the first time to the term entrepreneur. So much so that his work "Essei sur la Nature du commerce en Gèneral" (Cantillon, 1755) is considered by many to be the first attempt in the history of entrepreneurship studies to describe the figure of the entrepreneur as a supporter of the risk associated with the execution of an economic activity.

A key component of Adam Smith's (1776) perspective is the idea of functions. Smith advocates the idea of the multifunction of entrepreneurs, i.e., as a capitalist-owner subject and as a combinator of productive elements, in contrast to Cantillon's earlier conception.

In reality, we discover the following in his book *The Wealth of Nation*: "*Thus, of the product of the land, one part replaces the capital of the farmer, the other pays his profit and the rent of landlord; and thus constitutes a revenue both to the owner of this capital and to some other personas the rent of his land*" (Smith, 1776, p. 123).

The major proponent of this strategy is F.H. Knight, in his article "Risk Uncertainty and Profit" (Knight, 1921), suggests an entrepreneurial vision that is quite similar to Cantillon's earlier vision from approximately two centuries prior.

According to Knight, the core of an entrepreneur's job is to make judgments under "uninsurable uncertainty" and "uninsurable risk" while also attempting to capitalize on future business prospects most likely.

2.1.3 Psychological Approach

The psychological approach to entrepreneurship studies encompasses the theoretical contributions that focus and deepen the reasons for the will and the entrepreneurial choices and the psychological and behavioral traits that characterize entrepreneurs.

In concrete terms, the origin of this approach can be traced back to the research of Schumpeter (1911). According to the scholar, to introduce innovations into the economic system, the entrepreneur must have some specific personal characteristics. Therefore, he should have a personality that allows him to manage risk, exercise leadership, be intuitive, and have an innate tendency toward problem solving.

After Schumpeter's contribution, the psychological approach is consolidated and acquires relevance with the introduction of the concept of "alertness" (Kirzner, 1973), that is, a state of alert that allows the entrepreneur to seize market opportunities that others have not yet cultured.

Other studies have focused on the desire for "independence" from other higher professional degrees and "ambition" to achieve success and social recognition and thus a need for prestige and self-realization (Maslow, 1943; McClelland, 1965; Davids, 1963).

This moment marks the passage in which many scholars have begun to focus the attention of their studies toward the concept of "entrepreneur psychology."

2.1.4 Multivocal Strategic Approach

While building on the findings of the earlier conventional approaches, the multidimensional approach to the study of the entrepreneur and, by extension, of entrepreneurship introduces fresh viewpoints that can be regarded as the primary inputs to studies of new entrepreneurship and start-up ecosystems.

Before moving on to an analysis of the most recent studies within this approach, some studies should be considered that, although not recent, can be considered precursors (Schumpeter, 1911; Drucker, 1985). Drucker made the following assumption in his book Innovation and Entrepreneurship: "INNOVATION" is the distinctive instrument of entrepreneurs, the technique by which they exploit change as an opportunity for a different firm or a different service. It is something that can be studied and practiced (p. 20). A blatant allusion to the idea that business owners must actively look for the seeds of successful innovation outside, on purpose. Therefore, the pursuit of possibilities already provides the groundwork for Drucker's vision, but it expands forcefully through a new strategy known as "strategic entrepreneurship" in the literature (Venkataraman & Sarasvathy, 2005; Sarasvathy, 2001). An entrepreneur is involved and motivated in the identification of an entrepreneurial opportunity, which must then be chosen and taken advantage of, claims this theoretical framework of strategic entrepreneurship.

According to strategic entrepreneurship, the phase of recognizing an entrepreneurial opportunity—which may happen in one of three ways: recognition, discovery, or creation—is the first step in the entrepreneurial process (Barney & Clark, 2007; Sarasvathy et al., 2008).

This contradicts the modern understanding of the entrepreneur based on these most recent frameworks. In fact, according to Sara Sarasvathy (2001), the latter can only use its cognitive talents to grasp specific business chances in uncertain and continuously changing situations since it no longer has a reference market to evaluate, anticipate, and regulate. Based on what is referred to as an "effectual logic" (Sarasvathy, 2001).

The environment in which the firm functions is a more recent integration that is closely tied to the research for this book. In any event, the latter affects the entrepreneur's behaviors, and this is true both in favorable circumstances (display of entrepreneurial vitality) and in hostile contexts, which might prompt the entrepreneur to take a proactive behavior precisely because of the challenges that occur (Bygrave, 2006).

Henry Chesbrough, a Californian economist, describes a strategic and cultural approach to innovation in which business owners should also employ resources from outside their company to produce more value and compete successfully (from start-ups, universities, institutions, etc.)

Chesbrough (2003) asserts that the paradigm of "closed innovation" has been completely replaced by that of "open innovation," in which possibilities are sought outside of the boundaries of the organization and owners need not worry about being the sole owners of innovations and their resources (Chesbrough, 2003).

Today's entrepreneurs must adapt to a complicated, global, and dynamic environment. The idea of entrepreneurship is redefined (Table 1).

Finally, it appears vital to point out several entrepreneur studies' limitations:

Table 1 Our Systematization of multidimensional approaches for the study of entrepreneurship

Approach	Author	Key focus
Historical approach	Marx	*Individual possessed by the lust for wealth*
Historical approach	Weber	*Individual driven by an almost transcendental vocation also of an ethical and religious type*
Historical approach	Parson	*Individual with specific social function*
Functional approach	Cantillon	*Individual other than the landowner and with operational functions*
Functional approach	Smith	*Individual who combines and transforms the factors of production*
Functional approach	Knight	*Individual who takes the risk*
Psychological approach	Schumpeter	*Individual who promotes innovation*
Psychological approach	Kirzner	*Opportunity sensitive individual*
Psychological approach	Maslow	*Individual aiming to scale the social ladder*
Multivocal approach (the basics)	Schumpeter/ Drucker	Innovation
MV/strategic approach	Sarasvathy S	Effectuation
MV/strategic approach	Chersbrough	Open innovation

Prior to researching entrepreneurship, we started off by studying the entrepreneur, but the fundamental issue was that we had any specific research questions for the entrepreneur.

Therefore, research on entrepreneurship as a complex phenomenon and a field of business administration has gained popularity in recent years rather than focusing on the individual entrepreneur. Because there are many specialized scientific publications as well as monographic materials, these studies currently provide a superior theoretical, methodological, and academic structure.

3 The New Entrepreneurship: Start-Up Companies

Innovative concepts that result in start-ups are expanding. Start-up businesses are expanding increasingly thanks to contemporary digital technology.

In the past 10 years, several academics have examined the expanding phenomenon of start-ups from a variety of perspectives. In recent years scholars have underestimated the significance of the creation of fresh, creative businesses, viewing them as only one aspect of the larger field of entrepreneurship research, if that (Frederiksen & Brem, 2017; Matricano, 2019).

Numerous literary works have examined start-up phenomena and attempted to explain what a start-up business is. It is a given that it is impossible to develop a concise, all-encompassing definition of a start-up. Many authors, including academics, business professionals, and investors, focus on the difficulties from various angles that emphasize various components in recognizing a start-up.

We have tried to organize how start-ups are defined in line with the Gartner and Katz theoretical framework (1988).

We have chosen three of the four properties proposed by Gartner and Katz to develop a structure that allows the identification of organizations in the early stages of their creation process: "Prospective Intention," "Resources & Activities," and "Relations with the environment."

3.1 Start-Up Definition with a Focus on "Future Intention"

Without fail, the phrase "start-up" should not be mistaken for an organization's start-up phase, which refers to the company's initial stage of development, during which the company is either bought and relaunched through a new start-up or is initially introduced to the market. On the other hand, some definitions (Drucker, 1985) overemphasize the idea of "correct thought," and even these, according to this study, are as wrong. Therefore, according to Edison (1989), "Genius is one percent inspiration and 99% perspiration."

Start-up businesses are young businesses that fight for survival, while during the early stages, the entrepreneur takes the initiative to start several actions to develop his or her concept into a successful firm (Salamazadeh, 2015). The study of this work is particularly well suited to several of the start-up firm definitions that are most often used in the literature. In fact, a commonly used definition describes a start-up as a transitory firm used to find a "repeatable and scalable business model" (Blank, 2017). The words "temporary" and "search" should be underlined since a start-future up's involves either ceasing to be a start-up and joining a large corporation or failing and moving on to another opportunity. In fact, the difference between a start-up and a small business is that the latter is not capable of this type of rapid scale and probably does not even go toward this goal. The term "scalable business model" in this case means a business that can increase its size (and therefore its customers and turnover) exponentially without using.

In this context, a firm with a scalable business strategy is one that can grow exponentially in size (and therefore, in its clientele and revenue) "proportional resources" (Di Bernardo et al., 2021).

A scalable business model should be duplicated with few adjustments in many times and environments.

To enable this type of growth, digital transformation with new discoveries, software, and algorithms is crucial.

Companies such as Facebook, Google, Skype, and Airbnb have discovered a repeatable and scalable business model; as a result, they are no longer start-ups but rather established businesses. A start-up's main objective is to stop being a start-up, either by rapidly growing into a huge company or by failing and moving on to new prospects.

3.2 *Start-Up Definition with a Focus on "Resources"*

Eric Ries, the inventor of the Lean Start-up process, refocuses attention on the human element. Start-ups are "human institutions built to provide a novel product or service under conditions of high uncertainty," according to Ries (Ries, 2011, p. 27). Thus, it becomes obvious that the word "human institution" is being emphasized. More precisely, starting from this definition, it is possible to identify the start-up with what it does, referring to its product or service, forgetting that part of its value is in its organizational culture, which is a core element of all great ex-start-ups. Start-ups are experiments on platforms that test possible automatizations both in business and in daily life. Start-ups tend to apply known techniques to new processes. Success and failure reasons depend on many different and combined elements. In fact, Marmer et al. (2011) claim that start-ups must develop *a 5-week strategy* to offer a product or service designed to satisfy user needs and that start-ups are continuously developing organizations, operating along five interdependent areas: customer, product, team, business model, and financials (Marmer et al., 2011).

3.3 *Start-Up Definition with a Focus on "Relations between the Environment and High Risk"*

The "post-entry" trend of start-ups, or the outcomes attained or achievable by new businesses that employ and exploit innovation and technology, has received the most attention in recent years (Sorrentino, 2003), and this trend has been studied in detail (Decker et al., 2016).

Italian academics and practitioners are increasingly looking to the phenomena of start-up businesses as a solution to the country's numerous issues with unemployment and economic decline (Matricano, 2019). We cannot use the concepts of inherent risk while analyzing the external elements that affect the creation and longevity of start-ups. Innovation may lead to superior performance and substantial financial gains. High risk is engaged in the atmosphere of severe uncertainty in which innovation occurs and start-ups expand (Ries, 2011).

Paul Graham, an American essayist, developer, start-up founder, and CEO of Y Combinator, one of the most effective start-up accelerators, believes that a company can only experience rapid growth if it produces a product that a wide range of customers are interested in and is able to reach and serve the entire large market. A start-up differs from a small firm in that the former has rapid growth and business scalability (Graham, 2012).

The true start-up, which does not replicate or create a script but instead creates something entirely novel and then compares it to uncertain conditions by going where no one has gone before, serves as the benchmark for emergency situations.

4 The Legislative Framework in Italy: *"Start-Up Innovativa"*

In Italy, in 2012, the D.L. 179/2012 introduced some specific measures to support this type of business during its life cycle (birth, growth, maturity). With this regulation, in addition to developing a dynamic and competitive innovation ecosystem, creating new opportunities for doing business, and promoting employment, the legislature wanted to promote a sustainable growth strategy. Companies that meet the requirements can self-certify that they meet the criteria for innovative start-ups and qualify for the advantages by registering in the relevant part of the Register of Companies at their province's Section of Commerce. Within 5 years of their existence, innovative start-ups can experience the anticipated benefits; beyond this time, they have the option to transition into innovative SMEs without losing the benefits that are now accessible.

Pursuant to relevant legislation (Legislative Decree 179/2012, Art. 25, paragraph 2, an innovative start-up is a joint-stock company also established in cooperative form, which meets the following objective requirements (MISE, 2021):

- It has a residence in Italy or in another country of the European Economic Area but with a production site or branch in Italy.
- New business or one that has not yet been around for 5 years.
- Its annual turnover must be less than 5 million euros.
- It must not have produced profits for its members.
- It is not listed on a multilateral trading platform or on a regulated exchange.
- It has as its exclusive or prevailing corporate purpose the development, production, and marketing of a product or service with high technological value.
- Neither a merger, a spin-off, nor the sale of a business unit produced it.
- Finally, a start-up qualifies as innovative if at least one of the following three arbitrary criteria is met:

(1) Possesses highly qualified staff (at least one-third PhDs, PhD students, or researchers, or at least two-third with master's degrees); (2) incurs R&D and innovation expenses equal to at least 15% of the higher value between turnover and cost of production; and (3) is the owner, custodian, or licencee of at least one patent or owner of a registered software.

The list of concessions allowed by Italian law for businesses that are able to obtain special registration with the Italian business director is listed below. (Registro delle imprese, 2021). In Italy, innovative start-ups are subject to measures beginning on the date of their registration in the special area and for a maximum of 5 years after the date of their founding.

Additionally, the decree-law of May 19, 2020, n. 34 (also known as the "Relaunch" Decree), provided provisions to assist and enhance the ecosystem of creative entrepreneurs.

The list of allowances for creative start-ups is shown below:

- Digital and free constitution of the start-up.
- Tax incentives for investment in the capital of innovative start-ups.
- Free and simplified access to the Guarantee Fund for SMEs.
- Smart & Start Italy (subsidized loans for innovative start-ups located on the national territory).
- Seamless transformation into innovative SMEs.
- Exemption from chamber rights and stamp duties.
- Raising capital through equity crowdfunding campaigns.
- Business internationalization services (ICE).
- Exceptions to ordinary corporate regulations.
- Discipline of flexible work.
- Extension of the deadline for covering losses.
- Derogation from the regulation on shell companies and systematic loss companies.
- Remuneration through equity participation instruments.
- Exemption from the obligation to affix the compliance visa for offsetting VAT credits.
- Fail Fast (simplified procedures in case of failure of your business).

These norms, through subsequent measures, have significantly favored the growth of Italian start-up businesses in recent years. The 2022 statistics speak for themselves:

- Nearly 15 K Start-Ups (6% of all the registered capital companies in Italy).
- 65 K Workers.
- 765,000 shareholders.
- Turnover 180 k (on average).
- Two billion dollars were raised (2022) (Registro delle imprese, 2022).

5 Discussion

The diffusion of the phenomenon of start-up companies in Italy reflects what is also happening globally. In the economies of many countries around the world, start-ups are considered fundamental players. We speak of start-up ecosystems precisely to underline the fact that the latter, during their development, involves a plurality of interlocutors such as large companies, local institutions, and organizations aimed at supporting the latter. Even if the phenomenon is gradually expanding throughout the world, it takes on very different characteristics from country to country depending on the different latitudes. Italy has witnessed the birth of a national regulation that has undoubtedly fomented the birth of new start-up companies, but the strong lag compared to other countries of the world in terms of investment funds is still being discounted. Venture capitalists should be encouraged to invest in start-ups even more than is happening. New technologies, as will be described later, have a strong influence on the proliferation of startup ecosystems. The strong gap will be highlighted in the last chapter, where the author reports a benchmarking activity that compares the Italian start-up ecosystems with the excellent ones from overseas such as Silicon Valley. The author proposes, through the subsequent chapters of the monograph, to shed light on the scenario just mentioned.

References

Barney, J. B., & Clark, D. N. (2007). *Resource-based theory: Creating and sustaining competitive advantage*. OUP Oxford.

Blank, S. (2017). Why the lean start-up changes everything. *Harvard Business Review*.

Bygrave, W. D. (2006). *The entrepreneurship paradigm, handbook of qualitative research in entrepreneurship*. Edward Elgar Publishing Inc..

Cantillon, R. (1755). *An essay on commerce in general*. History of Economic Thought Books.

Chesbrough, H. W. (2003). *Open innovation: The new imperative for creating and profiting from technology*. Harvard Business School Press.

Ciappei, C., Schillaci, S., & Tani, S. (2006). *Gli incubatori di impresa, esperienze internazionali a confronto*. University Press.

Corley, K., & Gioia, D. A. (2011). Building theory about theory building: What constitutes a theoretical contribution? *The Academy of Management Review, 36*, 12–32.

Davids, L. (1963). *Characteristics of small business founder in Texas and Georgia*. University of Georgia, Athens.

Decker, R., Haltiwanger, J., Jarimin, R., & Miranda, J. (2016). Where has all the skewness gone? The decline in high-growth (Young) firms in the U.S. *European Economic Review, 86*.

Di Bernardo, I., Tregua, M., Fabio, G., & Andrea, R. (2021). *AI as a boost for startups companies: Evidence from Italy* (Vol. 5, p. 53). University of South Florida. *(USF) M3 Publishing*.

Drucker, P. (1985). *Innovation and entrepreneurship. Practice and principles*. Harper& Row Publishers.

Edison, T. (1989). "What is genius". Quote from an interview from the Harpers Monthly interview.

Frederiksen, D. L., & Brem, A. (2017). How do entrepreneurs think they create value? A scientific reflection of Eric Ries' Lean Start-up approach. *International Entrepreneurship and Management Journal, 13*(1), 169–189.

Gartner, W., & Katz, J. (1988). Properties of Emerging Organizations. *The Academy of Management Review, 13*(2), 429–441.

Graham, P. (2012). *Start-up = growth*. Internet access. http://www.paulgraham.com/growth.html, 1.

Hirsch, J. M. (2011). Employee or Entrepreneur. *Wash. & Lee L. Rev., 68*, 353.

Kirzner, I. M. (1973). *Competition and Entrepreneurship and Economic Development*. University of Chicago press.

Knight, F. H. (1921). Cost of production and price over long and short periods. *Journal of political economy, 29*(4), 304–335.

Kuratko, D. F., & Audretsch, D. B. (2009). Strategic entrepreneurship: exploring different perspectives of an emerging concept. *Entrepreneurship theory and practice, 33*(1), 1–17.

MacMillan, I. C., & Katz, J. A. (1992). Idiosyncratic milieus of entrepreneurial research: The need for comprehensive theories. *Journal of Business Venturing, 7*(1), 1–8.

Marmer, M., Herrmann, B. L., Dogrultan, E., Berman, R., Eesley, C., & Blank, S. (2011). Start-up genome report extra: Premature scaling. *Start-up genome, 10*, 1–56.

Marx, K. (1964). *Edizione italina del "Il Capitale"*. Editori Riuniti.

Maslow, A. H. (1943). A theory of human motivation. *Psychological Review, 50*(4), 370–396.

Matricano, D. (2015). *Lo studio dell'Impreditorialità, un approccio di indagine multidimensionale*. Carrocci Editori.

Matricano D. (2019), Lo studio dell'imprenditorialità,. Carrocci Editore.

McClelland, D. C. (1965). Toward a theory of motive acquisition. *American Psychologist, 20*(5), 321–333.

MISE. (2021). Requirements for official registration as an Italian innovative startup. From the website of the Italian company register.

Okhuysen, G., & Bonardi, J. P. (2011). Editors 'comments: The challenges of building theory by combining lenses. *The Academy of Management Review, 36*, 6–11.

Parsons, T., & Smelser, N. J. (1956). *Economy and society*. Free Press.

Ries, E. (2011). *The lean start-up: How today's entrepreneurs use continuous innovation to create radically successful businesses*. Currency.

Salamazadeh. (2015). *Start-up companies: Life cycle and challenges*.

Sarasvathy, S. (2001). Causation and Effectuation: Toward a theoretical shift from economic inevitability to entrepreneurial contingency. *Academy of Management Review, 26*(2).

Sarasvathy, S., et al. (2008). Designing organizations that design environments: lesson from entrepreneurial expertise. *Organization studies*, 331–350.

Schumpeter, J. A. (1911). *The theory of economic development*. Harvard University Press.

Smith, A. (1776). An inquiry into the nature and causes of the wealth of nations: Volume One.. printed for W. Strahan; and T. Cadell, 1776.

Sorrentino, M. (2003). *LE nuove imprese*. Economia delle nuove imprese imprese imprenditoriali.

Timmons, J. A., Spinelli, S., & Tan, Y. (2004). *New venture creation: Entrepreneurship for the twenty-first century* (Vol. 6). McGraw-Hill/Irwin.

Venkataraman, S., & Sarasvathy, S. D. (2005). Strategy and entrepreneurship: Outlines of an untold story. *The Blackwell handbook of strategic management*, 655–673.

Weber, M. (1904). *L'etica protestante e lo spirito del capitalismo*. Sansoni Editori.

Wiklund, J., Davidsson, P., Audretsch, D. B., & Karlsson, C. (2011). The future of entrepreneurship research. *Entrepreneurship Theory and Practice, 35*(1), 1–9.

The Support Mechanisms for Innovative Entrepreneurship: Start-up Accelerators and Incubators

1 The Origins of Support Programs for New Businesses

The relationship between innovation and the emergence of new enterprises and economic growth has been steadily built over time, beginning in the 1940s with the introduction of Schumpeter's idea of creative destruction. Thus, there is a growing acceptance of the idea of fostering the development of new, creative businesses (Bruneel et al., 2012).

The phenomenon of business incubators and start-ups is today as never in the past under the attention of public opinion and national governments. With reference to this statement, consider the Start-up America1 initiative, a program promoted by the Obama government, in January 2017, aimed at encouraging the American private sector to invest in start-up companies and small businesses in general. The program's primary initiatives include the creation of a $2 billion fund (distributed over 5 years) to assist the emergence of new entrepreneurial activities, the elimination of the capital gains tax for small enterprises, and the acceleration of the patent registration process. According to the National Business Incubator Association, the first example of a business incubator dates to 1959 in the city of Batavia, New York state. As specified in the NBIA report, the Batavia Industrial Center represented the first attempt to aid services to newly founded companies through the provision of shared services. Only around the end of the 1970s did the phenomenon of incubators start to take on serious relevance in the United States (Knopp, 2007). As understanding of how this tool may represent a real contribution to regional economic growth grew after those years, comparable programs were also developed inside the European Union. Paul Graham, a former entrepreneur turned angel investor, developed the initial idea for an accelerator in Boston and Silicon Valley in 2005. Brad Feld and David Cohen founded the second accelerator (Tech Stars), which has a very similar character, in Boulder in 2007 with the goal of fostering regional growth while providing more active ("hands-on") support for entrepreneurs. These two

F. Greco, *Startup Ecosystems*, Studies on Entrepreneurship, Structural Change and Industrial Dynamics, https://doi.org/10.1007/978-3-031-34414-5_3

accelerators quickly became benchmarks to be followed, inspiring hundreds of similar programs worldwide (Salido et al., 2013).

In 2012, the NBIA estimated that there were 7000 facilities worldwide and approximately 1250 business incubators in the United States (data NBIA October 2012).

A total of 364 incubation programs that took part in the World Benchmark 2019–2020 were categorized and analyzed for the 2020 UBI Global World Rankings of Business Incubators and Accelerators.

2 Current Scenario: UBI Global World Rankings of Business Incubators and Accelerators

In 2022, UBI GLOBAL conducted one of the world's most comprehensive studies and benchmarks of business incubators and accelerators in 2021–2022. Swedish research firm UBI Global specializes in providing research services. For corporations and incubators, benchmarking, rating, and matching. The effectiveness and impact of business incubators and accelerators are examined in the World Benchmark Study 2021–2022. Studying participating programs are four different groups: corporate, university, public, and private.

The latest "Word ranking 2019/20 by UBI Global" edited by the head of researcher Holger Meyer was drawn up in the context of UBI GLOBAL activities. The research focused on 1580 initiatives from all over the world, including incubators and accelerators. A total of 591 programs that responded to the audit and only 364 programs from 78 countries were included in the ranking. The evaluated topics were divided into incubators and accelerators, with a focus on university efforts, company-managed initiatives, and public administration initiatives. As a result, the following categories emerged:

- University Business incubator/accelerator that derives its business objectives primarily from one or more universities, by which it is o en operated and primarily nanced.
- "Public" Business incubator/accelerator that derives its business objectives primarily from one or more public entities by which it is operated and primarily networked.
- Private Business incubator/accelerator that develops its business objectives largely independently, o end operates autonomously and primarily nuances its own operations.
- Corporate Business incubator/accelerator that derives its business objectives primarily from one or more for-pro t corporations, by which it is o o end operated and primarily nanced (Fig. 1).

The KPIs listed below serve as the foundation for the seven subcategory scores, which in turn create the scores in the three main categories listed below, which are

fundamental support role because they provide a facility where the personnel of incubator firms can come together, interact and mobilize resources."

- Cohen (2013) used multiple case studies of nine accelerators in the United States to assess "how organizational learning occurs and accelerate new venture creation in such time-compressed programs. Among the key findings in this work, the author highlights the importance of four components in the learning/new venture creation process in accelerators: (i) mentor overload, (ii) accelerator director expertise, (iii) learning in divided teams, and (iv) cohort peer learning. The results suggest that time compression enhances learning (contrary to previous theoretical predictions), firms delay "doing" until strategy emerges and begins to stabilize, teams dividing each member's area of expertise enhance overall organizational learning, ventures accelerated in the same cohort (regardless of any industry focus) improve their aspirational goals and expand founders' overall capabilities and knowledge, and finally it suggests that concentration of expertise among focal firms matters, in particular the knowledge transfer by accelerator directors to start-ups" (Cohen, 2013).
- Cohen and Hochberg (2014) provide a first attempt to define not only what an incubator or accelerator is but more specifically what an acceleration program is, highlighting the difference between other programs intended to support start-ups.
- Dee et al. (2015) present a literature review focused on classification of acceleration programs based on different criteria, i.e., how the programs are funded and at what stage the programs intervene in the start-up training process.
- Ciappei et al. group incubators into two macro categories: nonprofit and profit-oriented. The nonprofit category includes science and technology parks, business innovation centers, and university incubators. Corporate business incubators and independent private incubators belong to the profit-oriented category (Ciappei et al., 2016).
- Greco and Tregua (2022) offer an overview of the determining variables that allow incubators and accelerators to support start-up companies. The authors propose a focus on university incubators, which in recent years are increasingly spreading as a model (Table 7).

4 How Accelerators Work?

Many have offered classifications of start-up company accelerators and incubators based on many factors, both academics and practitioners (Aernoudt, 2004; Grimaldi & Grandi, 2005; Bruneel et al. (2012); Cohen, 2013).

The purpose of this paragraph is to clearly differentiate between the concepts of incubator and accelerator while also outlining our classification based on the latter's operational models.

Modern incubator and accelerator models are distinct from one another in terms of process and, more importantly, because they have dissimilar aims, practices and

Table 7 Summary of four main conceptualizations of the literature on incubators

Author	Research question	Methodology	Findings
Aernoudt (2004)	Among the different forms of support which of these should a start-up accelerator offer more?	Studies.	Depending on the market conditions and the context in which they are inserted, an accelerator should offer ways to access new markets.
Bruneel et al. (2012)	What evolution of functions have the accelerators of start-up companies had over time?	Data collected within seven BIs and their tenants regarding service provision and selection criteria.	Findings show that while BIs of all generations offer similar support services, tenants in older generation BIs make less use of the BI's service portfolio.
Cohen (2013)	How can firms accelerate learning? And broadly, how entrepreneurship can be taught?	Qualitative multiple case studies of nine accelerators in the United States to assess how organizational learning occurs and accelerate new venture creation in such time-compressed programs.	Accelerator programs do accelerate start-ups Earning through four major components—(i) mentor expertise transfer overload, (ii) accelerator director expertise transfer, (iii) learning through divided teams, and (iv) learning through cohort peers.
Greco and Tregua (2022)	What are the determining variables of academic incubators?	The authors adopted a qualitative approach (Dubois & Gadde, 2002) due to the nature of the topic being basically related to the features of UBAs and the novelty of the debate	UBAs offer a hard-to-replicate combination of suitable conditions for start-up acceleration, due to prestige in the business context, the operationalization of models and methods, and the setting up of a fertile ground for start-ups.

workflows. The following categorization is in line with the classification established by Aernoudt (2004) many years ago, and it is based on three basic aims:

(a) *Model 1: To support start-ups to participate in future economic results.*
(b) *Model 2: To diffuse innovation process and the new entrepreneurial culture in regional and local ecosystems.*
(c) *Model 3: To support start-ups for the integration of social categories.*

M. (A)-Typical incubators/accelerators with this goal are private incubators. In this case, the business model consists of the creation and rapid development of small businesses arising from entrepreneurial ideas. The incubator receives a share of the start-capital ups in return for the services it renders to the incubated companies (from the conception to the validation of the business model, the assistance of expert management, the provision of basic services such as PR, HR, legal advice, and inclusion in contact networks). Broadly speaking, it is possible to identify two types of private incubators: corporate business incubators (CBIs) and independent business incubators (IBIs). The substantial difference is the fact that the former are internal realities of large companies that choose this configuration to manage research and development projects, and in some cases give rise to spin-offs, or projects that arise from corporate resources (financial but above all know-how) and end up becoming independent entities that help diversify the corporate strategy. IBIs, on the other hand, are typical investment fund businesses that offer small sums of venture capital to start-ups searching for seed money and support their growth through a range of services. They have been a part of their development since the company was founded. Firm occasionally leading to a public market IPO. In essence, these are just financial tools, and often, their use is exhausted when other kinds of lenders enter the picture.

Knopp (2007) proposes for summary purposes an indicative list of the main types of services provided by the typical private business incubator.

- Access to Angel Investors and Venture Capital
- High-speed Internet access
- Marketing and business planning assistance
- Assistance in the marketing of technology
- Assistance in training the management team
- Networking activities
- Links to strategic partners
- Management of intellectual property
- Coaching and improvement of presentation techniques
- Accounting, financial management, and legal assistance services

M. (B)-The second type of incubator identified is that related to University Business Incubators (UBI).

The UBIs' primary objectives are similar to those of new entrepreneurial culture and innovation dissemination in regional and local ecosystems. These types of incubators are usually public structures where the university is often a member of the organization or, in any case, is highly integrated with universities. One of the first contributions on UBAs framed them—as well as university-based incubators—as entities supporting "entrepreneurial teams during the early stage" (Stayton & Mangematin, 2016); a restrictive approach to UBAs was preferred by Breznitz and Zhang (2019), who described them as an organization supporting firms' growth with specific reference to "graduates' development as entrepreneurs" (p. 868). UBAs are part of a regional entrepreneurial ecosystem, in addition to often being connected to time-limited programs (Mansoori et al., 2019). The focus of the latter is mainly concentrated on the transmission of technological knowledge to companies, favoring, e.g., academic spin-offs. In this case, university incubators pursue the aforementioned objectives through an action in particular: or the reduction in the reduction of the "discovery gap" (Meyer et al., 2011), that is, the distance that separates a scientific discovery from its application on the market. The technologies developed here are used as new businesses or are limited to the commercial exploitation of discoveries through royalties generated by licenses. The services that these structures provide are essentially of 2 types: services typical of incubators and services relating to the world of university research. Private incubators and UBIs, despite the support they have always received from European governments, have often been criticized because their respective results are not immediately measurable.

In the next chapter, when we address the issue of the influence of institutions on the start-up ecosystem, we will focus in particular on the role of the university and therefore of university incubators.

M. (C)-The incubators and the accelerators with this lat goal—c—are the social incubators.

The first's goal is to close the social gap by taking measures to make it easier for individuals with less education or experience—such as disabled individuals, unskilled employees, and long-term jobless individuals—to obtain jobs. Thus, the integration of social categories and the establishment of employment are the goals of the last type of incubation path outlined (Arnoudt, 2004). Most of the time, this kind of incubator assists start-ups or nonprofit projects around social innovation (Sentana et al., 2017; Sansone et al., 2020). Sansone et al. (2020), in particular, highlight the characteristics that differentiate social incubators from generic incubators and accelerators. The highlights of their research findings are that the social incubator (SI) is focused on start-ups with a significant social impact and that SIs give more attention to social impact measurements compared to other incubators. The same authors confirm that SIs are as efficient as other incubators in terms of tenants' growth (Table 8).

Table 8 Author's reworking of the Arnoudt table (2004) relating to the classes of incubators and related areas of activity, functions, and objectives

Types/ Mission-objectives-functions	Mission	Main goals	Sector involved
Private Incubator	ROI	Create Successful start-ups	All sectors
University Incubator	Disseminating entrepreneurial culture at the local level and optimizing the discovery gap	Spin-offs and technology transfer	Above Hi-Tech
Social Incubator	Social gap	Integration of social categories and employment creation	No profit sector/social innovation
Mixed Incubator	A mix of the elements mentioned	A mix of the goals mentioned	All sectors

4.1 *Analyzing the Differences between Start-Up Incubator and Start-Up Accelerator*

Many practitioners and scholars use the terms incubator and accelerator as if they were synonyms. On the surface, the two realities may seem very similar and, in this work, we too have often referred to them with the same term "incubators" but in reality they hide differences between the two terms, especially with the spread of the phenomenon.

Several entrepreneurship scholars have focused on the differences between the two realities (Cohen, 2013; Sepulveda, 2012; Isabelle, 2013; Tripathi & Oivo, 2020). The most important certainly concerns the type of companies that become part of the incubator and accelerator and the stage in which these occur. The incubator is aimed at start-ups that in many cases are not yet born or are in an early stage that can only be accessed with the presentation of a good idea. On the accelerator, on the other hand, start-ups that have already started and need a boost to continue to grow to enter the accelerator. In this last case, the selection is much more competitive.

> Incubators tend to nurture nascent ventures by buffering them from the environment to give them room to grow. In contrast, whereas accelerators speed up market interactions to help nascent ventures adapt quickly and learn (Cohen, 2013 p. 21).

In particular, according to Cohen (2013), accelerators and incubators differ in four keyways:

1. *Duration.*

Duration is the feature that most clearly distinguishes acceleration programs from incubation programs. The acceleration path is usually 3 months. Research on incubators suggests that companies graduate from incubators 1 to 5 years after inception.

2. *Relationship of "cohorts."*

Different relationships arise between the founders of the start-ups and the members of the accelerator or incubator (The Cohort).

Accelerator members and start-up founders (often belonging to investment funds) become very close by helping and motivating each other during the program, almost as if they were colleagues from the same company.

In different ways, incubator members can also develop relationships, and the experience of starting the program at the same time fosters unusually strong bonds and feelings and a common identity among the founders.

Susan Choen asked the founders of the company what their relationships were with the other members of their cohort. One said they would do "*anything for those guys.*"

3. *Business Model.*

Most of the original accelerators are privately owned and take an equity stake in the initiatives that participate in the programs. Additionally, some accelerator managers are also active angel investors who provide additional funding to some of the ventures, either directly or through a fund. Incubators, on the other hand, are mostly publicly owned, managed by managers and generally do not have their own investment funds. This implies that the managers of accelerators who are also the investors in the companies they are helping are more incentivized and aligned to the initiatives than are the managers of professional incubators.

Additionally, some accelerator owners have extensive previous experience as entrepreneurs or angel investors, giving them first-hand experience as start-up founders.

"Accelerators want growth that leads to a positive exit, while the best outcome for an incubator may be slower growth, which delays graduation and prolongs the tenant status of the firm" (Cohen, 2013 p 22).

4. *Selection.*

The start-up selection process is another important difference between incubators and accelerators. Accelerators select start-ups in batches, usually once or twice a year, while incubators accept new initiatives all the time.

The sales metrics and the product development stage must be in an advanced state for accelerators, while earlier stages are fine for incubators.

In addition to the three key differences identified by Choen, we also consider it important to detect and add a very important difference feature such as that of the Training and Mentorship process, which in the incubator is generic and basic support, while in the business accelerator, they are made available to mentorship courses and the assistance of specialized tutors who often support start-ups in the crucial fundraising phases and therefore in the financial economic evaluation of the start-ups.

5 Start-Up Valuation

In this historical period, the start-up evaluation issue is a highly popular topic. The founder's understanding of the start-value up is a prerequisite for achieving several goals. Undoubtedly connected to fundraising activity is the need to have a precise understanding of the start-up's evaluation.

The questions that start-up company founders frequently ask are as follows: *How much are the shares of my company now worth? How much money must be invested in the start-up by different types of investors to join the cape table?*

Even at the time of the start-foundation up's and as it moves from the stage of the business idea to the early phases of execution, evaluating the start-up is a highly delicate topic. Start-ups that enroll in acceleration and incubation programs with cap tables that are entirely out of balance and difficult to correct before adding new members are not a unique instance (Federico II Start up Valuation webinar, Microsoft Teams).

Incubators, important actors in today's start-up ecosystems, should unquestionably assist start-up founders in developing a clear understanding of the value of their start-up. The finance literature offers many suggested methods to estimate the value of a start-up:

There are economic methods that correspond to valuation methods that infer the value of the company's economic capital from the presumed value assigned to the expected company profits (Paganelli, 1990; Sonnier et al., 2007). These methods, in essence, calculate economic capital according to the company's income capacity.

After that, there are equity valuation methods that are based on the principle of analytical valuation of the individual elements of the assets and liabilities that make up the capital (Guatri, 1990). These systems, therefore, identify the value of the company in the book equity, obtained from the difference between the assets and liabilities of the company capital.

Finally, there are the most modern and transversal financial methods using a multiplicity of factors that are not tangible but also intangible for the evaluation of the value of start-ups such as that of the Score Card Method (Payne, 2011).

The latter appears to be a qualitative assessment method and is therefore considered more complete than the previous ones.

The scorecard method compares the target company to typical angel-funded start-up ventures and adjusts the average valuation of recently funded companies in the region to establish a premoney valuation of the target.

Such comparisons can only be made for companies at the same stage of development, in this case, for prerevenue start-up ventures.

> The Score Card Method is also very "simple to use and particularly suitable for start-ups in the early stage where making evaluations can be very risky" (Webinar Start up Valuation University Federico II of Naples).

Banca Intesa San Paolo uses the Score Card Method to evaluate projects, and the factors that it takes into consideration and that it measures through a score for every single item are the following:

1. Team: Competence and adequacy
2. Value proposition: Product/service potential offered, technology used, project feasibility, execution capacity
3. Market Opportunity: Originality, Tam/Sam/Som
4. Competition: Direct and indirect competitors
5. Business Pitch and Stage of development: Maturity, traction, Metrics
6. Investment requirements: Sustainability, use of the funds raised (Gruppointesasanpaolo.com)

From the description of the evaluation methods of a start-up, there are many factors that must be taken into consideration when estimating the value of a start-up. What stands out is that the classical methods pay much attention to tangible elements and little attention to intangible elements; in contrast, more modern and transversal methods give much importance to intangible elements. In this regard, it is important to refer to the concept of "human capital."

From several studies emerges the critical role of the composition of the team of founders in the possibility of acquiring investments (Muzyka et al., 1996). Following an analysis of the criteria used by some ventures.

US capitalists in the selection of investments, it can be said that the creation of a balanced team, or rather heterogeneous in its composition (Vanaelst et al., 2006).

By heterogeneity of the team, we mean, in this case, subjects who have different skills to deal with each of different functions. This makes the degree of execution certainly more performing and achievable.

5.1 *Fundraising: Stages of Start-Up Financing*

The many finance phases that are crucial for start-up business growth and connected to one another to the succession of the latter's progress will be examined in this paragraph (Capizzi et al., 2010; Klačmer Čalopa et al., 2014). In most circumstances, when we discuss start-up finance, we speak to risk capital rather than debt capital. The first refers to the capital (typically money, but, if necessary, it could also be composed of the grant of services or work in exchange for equity) that is given by an actor outside of the start-up and, as a result, allows this third party to join the shareholder structure (i.e., he becomes your partner) and, as a result, participate in the business risk as well as future financial results.

The second type of capital, called debt capital, is just a quantity of money that is deposited into the start-up's current account by a person or a financial institution. The start-up must return the money within a certain time frame, but it may occasionally obtain advantageous terms for doing so.

We track several investor actors' figures concurrently at each stage of fundraising, which we shall go into more detail below.

> Venture funding works like gears. A typical start-up goes through several rounds of funding, and at each round you want to take just enough money to reach the speed where you can shift into the next gear (Babych, "Splitting the Pie", LinkedIn, 2005).

5.1.1 Idea: Co-Founder Stage

> ...At first it is just you. You are pretty brilliant, and out of the many ideas you have had, you finally decide that this is the one.... As you start to transform your idea into a physical prototype, you realize that you can truly use another person's skills. So you look for a co-founder. However, you can't pay her any money (Grahm P., 2005).

To get from the concept to the implementation as rapidly as feasible during this stage, one surrounds themselves with co-founders who, rather than having financial resources, have the necessary talents to minimize the "*time to market*" as much as possible. At this point, there is still little emphasis on meeting financial necessities. A crucial phase is the shift from the idea to the implementation. Many would-be entrepreneurs had brilliant ideas, but they lacked the skills to put them into action. It is impossible to avoid mentioning Thomas Edinson (1903), an American inventor, businessman, and economist who once quipped, "Genius is 1% inspiration and 91% perspiration." His well-known adage changed over time.

5.1.2 Family and Friends Stage

With the initial funds received, the creators will be able to start working on the prototype of the idea and at the very least launch the alpha phase, which will test the same friends and family members together.

> You give him 5% of the company in exchange for $15,000 cash. Now you can afford room and ramen for another 6 months while building your prototype.

5.1.3 Seed Financing Stage

The start-ups implement an MVP, or Minimum Viable Product, at this phase (Lenarduzzi & Taibi, 2016). A method that falls between a product prototype and a marketing study entails building the most basic form of the project while keeping the core features—practically a Beta phase. Stop referring to it as a financial idea at this stage because a venture capitalist is already engaged in the experimentation phase.

There has not yet been proof of the product's or service's technological viability.

At this point, the company's idea is validated, and the largest loans, known as seed loans, start to arrive. The most popular methods for obtaining money are as follows:

- Investment funds that Incubators participate: The structures offer start-ups the first investments, a working environment and the support of professionals who collaborate in the supervision of the project and its validation phase in exchange for company shares.
- Crowdfunding: Bottom-up funding that leverages Internet fundraising. The project is posted on an online platform, and if it reaches the established goal, the person who submitted it receives the sum collected. Among the advantages of this tool is the possibility, through an excellent campaign, to create engagement with the product or service offered. Crowdfunding is at the same time also a marketing campaign because it gives the opportunity to describe all their projects, and everyone can sometimes participate in them with very small investments starting from 250 euros.
- Business Angels: Informal investors, start-up experts who invest relatively low sums (usually not above € 200,000) mainly in sectors such as digital technologies.

During the Seed Stage, therefore, the company is financed without the product or service to be offered having proven technical validity. This phase, together with the start-up phase, is part of the early stage.

5.1.4 Rounds (Series A-B...) Stage

Start-up funding Round A (First Stage Financing): Intervention during the productive activity's start-up phase when the commercial viability of the good or service has not yet been established. The issues in this instance are also mostly technical in nature, and the traits of the operators are similar to those in the prior instance.

However, compared to seed funding, the product has already been produced, although at the prototype stage, and the phases pertaining to any patents and engineering have passed. The requirements for launching a business are thus already in place since, often, the company already exists, the management has been created, and product tests and the necessary market research have been initiated. Financial resources are also needed at this time to support the growth of manufacturing and other commercial operations. Even start-up operations, which will be necessary operations such as, for example, the launch of new products and useful marketing activities to make themselves known on the markets by consumers, are particularly delicate for the future development possibilities of the company, as in the case of seed capital interventions.

Finance for expansion Round B: activities focused on fostering start-ups that have already attained a certain level of operational maturity and that are during production. The expansion or direct diversification of production capacity will take place throughout the development phase (Gualandri & Venturelli, 2011) (Fig. 2).

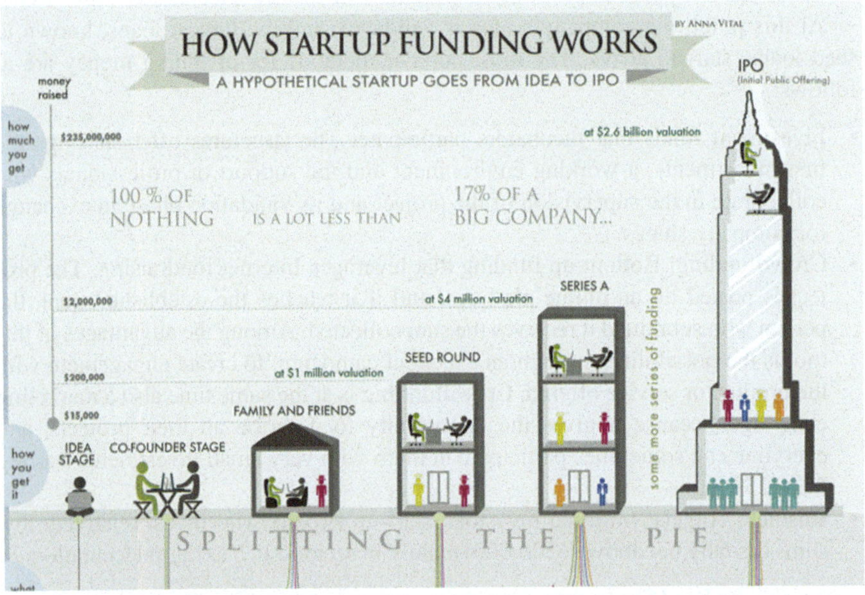

Fig. 2 Graphic representation: How Start-up Funding Works (www.paulgraham.com)

References

Aernoudt, R. (2004). Incubators: Tool for entrepreneurship? *Small Business Economics, 23*(2), 127–135.

Breznitz, S. M., & Zhang, Q. (2019). Fostering the growth of student start-ups from university accelerators: An entrepreneurial ecosystem perspective. *Industrial and Corporate Change, 28*(4), 855–873.

Bruneel, J., Ratinho, T., Clarysse, B., & Groen, A. (2012). The evolution of business incubators: Comparing demand and supply of business incubation services across different Incubator generations. *Technovation, 32*(2), 110–121.

Capizzi, V., Giovannini, R., Tirino, G., & Pesic, V. (2010). Business angels e informal venture capital in Italia.

Ciappei, C., Laudano, M. C., Zollo, L., & Rialti, R. (2016, September). Evaluating the quality of entrepreneurial education analysing its ability to increase entrepreneurial attitude and intent of students. In Toulon-Verona Conference Excellence in Services. ISO 690.

Cohen, S. (2013). What do accelerators do? Insights from incubators and angels. Innovations: Technology, Governance, Globalization, 8(3), 19–25.

Cohen, S., & Hochberg, Y. (2014). *Accelerating start-ups: The seed accelerator phenomenon.* Available at SSRN 2418000. Retrieved from http://papers.ssrn.com/sol3/Papers.cfm?abstract_id=2418000

Dee, N., Gill, D., Weinberg, C., & Mctavish, S. (2015). *Start-up support Programmes: What's the difference.*

Dubois, A., & Gadde, L. E. (2002). Systematic combining: An abductive approach to case research. *Journal of Business Research, 55*(7), 553–560.

Fukugawa, N. (2018). Is the impact of incubator's ability on incubation performance contingent on technologies and life cycle stages of start-ups?: Evidence from Japan. *The International Entrepreneurship and Management Journal, 14*, 457–478. https://doi.org/10.1007/s11365-017-0468-1

Greco, F., & Tregua, M. (2022). It gives you wheels: The university-based accelerators in start-up ecosystems. *International Journal of Entrepreneurship and Small Business, 45*(2), 235–257.

Grimaldi, R., & Grandi, A. (2005). Business incubators and new venture creation: An assessment of incubating models. *Technovation, 25*(2), 111–121.

Guatri L., La valutazione delle aziende. Teoria e pratica a confronto, 1990.

Gualandri E. & V. Venturelli, Nasce l'impresa, Business Angels: investitori a valore aggiunto, 2011.

Isabelle, D. (2013). Key factors affecting a technology entrepreneur's choice of incubator or accelerator. *Technology Innovation Management Review, 3*, 16–22.

Lenarduzzi, V., & Taibi, D. (2016, August). MVP explained: A systematic mapping study on the definitions of minimal viable product. In *2016 42th Euromicro Conference on Software Engineering and Advanced Applications (SEAA)* (pp. 112–119). IEEE.

Klačmer Čalopa, M., Horvat, J., & Lalić, M. (2014). Analysis of financing sources for start-up companies. *Management: Journal of Contemporary Management Issues, 19*(2), 19–44.

Knopp, L. (2007). *State of the business incubation industry.* National Business Incubation Association.

Mansoori, Y., Karlsson, T., & Lundqvist, M. (2019). The influence of the lean start-up methodology on entrepreneur-coach relationships in the context of a start-up accelerator. *Technovation, 84*, 37–47.

Mele C., Russo Spena T. (2019) Practising innovation, a sociomaterial view,. Editoriale Scientifica.

Meyer, A. D., Aten, K., Krause, A. J., Metzger, M. L., & Holloway, S. S. (2011). Creating a university technology commercialization programme: Confronting conflicts between learning, discovery, and commercialization goals. *International Journal of Entrepreneurship and Innovation Management, 13*(2), 179.

Muzyka, D., Birley, S., & Leleux, B. (1996). Trade-offs in the investment decisions of European venture capitalists. *Journal of Business Venturing, 11*(4), 273–287.

Paganelli, O. (1990). *Valutazione delle aziende*. UTET Università.

Payne, B. (2011). *Scorecard valuation methodology. Establishing the valuation of pre-revenue.*

Peters, L., Rice, M., & Sundararajan, M. (2004). The role of incubators in the entrepreneurial process. *The Journal of Technology Transfer, 29*(1), 83–91.

Salido, E., Sabás, M., & Freixas, P. (2013). *The accelerator and incubator ecosystem in Europe.*

Sansone, G., Andreotti, P., Colombelli, A., & Landoni, P. (2020). Are social incubators different from other incubators? Evidence from Italy. *Technological Forecasting and Social Change, 158*, 120132.

Scillitoe, J. L., & Chakrabarti, A. K. (2010). The role of incubator interactions in assisting new ventures. *Technovation, 30*(3), 155–167.

Sentana, E., González, R., Gascó, J., & Lopis, J. (2017). The social profitability of business incubators: A measurement proposal. *Entrepreneurship & Regional Development, 29*(1–2), 116–136.

Schwartz, M. (2008). Beyond incubation: An analysis of firm survival and exit dynamics in The PostGraduation period. *Journal Of Technological Transfer, 34*, 403–421.

Sepulveda, F. (2012). The difference between a business accelerator and a business incubator. *Inc Web, 31*, 1–14.

Soetanto, D. P., & Jack, S. L. (2013). Business incubators and the networks of technology-based firms. *The Journal of Technology Transfer, 38*(4), 432–453.

Sonnier, B. M., Carson, K. D., & Carson, P. P. (2007). Accounting for intellectual capital: The relationship between profitability and disclosure. *Journal of Applied Management and Entrepreneurship, 12*(2), 3.

Stayton, J., & Mangematin, V. (2016). Start-up time, innovation and organizational emergence: A study of USA-based international technology ventures. *Journal of International Entrepreneurship, 14*(3), 373–409.

Tripathi, N., & Oivo, M. (2020). The roles of incubators, accelerators, coworking spaces, mentors, and events in the start-up development process. In *Fundamentals of software start-ups* (pp. 147–159). Springer.

Vanaelst, I., Clarysse, B., Wright, M., Lockett, A., Moray, N., & S'Jegers, R. (2006). Entrepreneurial team development in academic spinouts: An examination of team heterogeneity. *Entrepreneurship Theory and Practice, 30*(2), 249–271.

Start-Up Ecosystems and Institutions: The Role of Universities and Academic Entrepreneurship

1 Key Players in the Start-Up Ecosystem: "The Innomediary"

Start-up businesses continually engage with innovation (Joshi & Satyanarayana, 2014; Bala Subrahmanya, 2017; Fraiberg, 2017), and since they operate in a multiactor environment, they are exposed to a variety of innovation carriers in addition to being innovators themselves. Researchers began to propose the idea of mediated innovation because of the focus of innovation studies on the agents and parties that carried and shared knowledge to promote innovation. First, Sawhney (2002) defined the third-party actors acting as mediators who facilitate innovation as "innomediaries." Additionally, they categorized them based on the firms they support and identified three actions, namely, connection, recombination, and dissemination of ideas to favor innovation. On the other hand, Vanhaverbeke and Cloodt (2014) framed innomediaries in the paradigm of open innovation; more specifically, they considered the advantages of mediation for innovation as favoring new trajectories of innovation and making innovation-oriented transactions more efficient. Similarly, Vanhaverbeke et al. (2014) questioned how a firm should be organized to get the most from innomediaries in terms of effectiveness. Furthermore, innomediaries are a new market actor favoring the cocreation of innovation, and the research by Mele and Russo-Spena (2015) described their role through a practice-based approach, highlighting engaging, exploring, exploiting, and orchestrating as ways to enable resource exchange and integration. Engaging is a way to build connections in social networks while exploring lever on knowledge and creativity in networks. This knowledge is fully exploited in the third practice through modifying and extending solutions, and finally orchestrating the definition of alignment and linkage of actors to achieve innovation and overcome the contextual divides. The practices defined by Mele and Russo-Spena (2015) can be found in many start-up ecosystems around the world described by the genome report referred to in the first chapter of this book (Table 1).

F. Greco, *Startup Ecosystems*, Studies on Entrepreneurship, Structural Change and Industrial Dynamics, https://doi.org/10.1007/978-3-031-34414-5_4

Table 1 The four practices in Genome Start-up Ecosystems: some evidence. Author's elaboration from multiple sources

Practices	Example 1	Example 2
Engaging	**Silicon Valley:** *Start-ups have access to talent (Stanford University, UC Berkeley, and USCF), capital, plus numerous investors, and mentors*	**Stockholm**: *Companies have access to top talent from some of Europe's top-ranking universities, such as the Stockholm School of Economics, Karolinska Institutet, and Royal Institute of Technology (KTH).*
Exploring	**Seattle:** *Microsoft and Amazon, both headquartered in the Seattle region, have been the source of numerous spin-off companies directly (such as Expedia). This record has given the region a rich genealogy of start-ups that become scaleups, be getting more start-ups.*	**Singapore:** *Singapore is rated as the second-best country to conduct business globally. Singapore now recognizes engineers are valued and should learn from Silicon Valley's practices.*
Exploiting	**Amsterdam:** *Start-ups can gain access to corporates across every sector. Nearly 200 multinationals have their European headquarters in Amsterdam, including Netflix, Uber, Tesla, and Salesforce.*	**Berlin:** *Berlin is home to more AI companies than any other German ecosystem and involves approximately 5000 people. However, the Berlin ecosystem attracts entrepreneurs and talent from all over the world and from different contexts, based on factors like essentials, openness, and recreation.*
Orchestrating	**Sidney:** *The region's many universities draw tens of thousands of international students, providing a* good *testing ground for Edtech start-ups. Sydney-based Smart Sparrow, an online learning design platform.*	**Singapore**: *Singapore is rated as the second-best country to conduct business globally.*

2 Entrepreneurship Education

Develop and promote education Entrepreneurship has been one of the key policy objectives of European institutions and member states for many years. In fact, in the context of youth with high unemployment rates, the economic crisis, and rapid changes due to the complexity of our economy and society based on knowledge, soft skills such as entrepreneurship are essential not only to shape the mentalities of young people but also to provide the skills, knowledge, and attitudes that are central to the development of one entrepreneurial culture in Europe. However, although some countries are already more than a decade committed to boosting entrepreneurship education, others are just leaving now. The European Commission recognizes that entrepreneurship education is a tool to help young people to be more entrepreneurial. It is about finding out how to develop a general skill set that applies to all areas of life, not just how to learn how to run a business (European Commission, 2022).

Naturally, international academic literature has also been interested in the topic. Several scholars have addressed academic entrepreneurship (Pittaway & Cope, 2007; Wilson, 2008; Consolini et al., 2013; Antonaci et al., 2014; Vanevenhoven, 2013). One of the first scientific approaches to the most important topic was that of Pittaway and Cope (2007), who explored different themes within entrepreneurship education using a systematic literature review. The findings of this in-depth literature review support the conclusion that entrepreneurship education has an impact on students' propensity and intentionality (Pittaway & Cope, 2007). The limitations of this study, which future studies will attempt to address, are the lack of evidence on how entrepreneurship education affects the level of entrepreneurship of future graduates or whether it enables graduates to become more effective entrepreneurs. A study that has more evident practical implications is that of Vanevenhoven (2013), who offers a contribution that has been taken into consideration by many scholars of entrepreneurship. It is a study on the necessary change of approach to guide future entrepreneurs who attend high school toward a more practical and implementing approach. He himself states that it is "his own interpretation" and should not be generalized but viewed with caution (Vanevenhoven, 2013).

A more recent contribution that combines the concept of entrepreneurial education with that of the well-being and proliferation of start-up ecosystems is that of Gupta (2023). This study investigates the impact of the university entrepreneurial ecosystem and entrepreneurship education on the initiation of new start-ups by students. Gupta (2023) uses an empirical random design approach to explore the causal relationship between independent and dependent variables. The scholar found that both independent variables (university education in entrepreneurship) positively and significantly influence the dependent variable (start-ups by students). Among the implications of this contribution, entrepreneurship education was considered the most influential factor with respect to the university entrepreneurial ecosystem (Gupta, 2023).

From the review of the literature on the topic of entrepreneurial education emerges that the scenario field of investigation of the studies (that confirm a positive trend in the dissemination of entrepreneurship education) very often refers to international contexts and very little to Italy. In fact, in Italy, although initiatives dedicated to youth policies have developed in recent years, training is dedicated to development of entrepreneurship, there are no real policies dedicated to entrepreneurial education and training. Consequently, 83% of Italian students aspire to an employee position immediately after graduation, while only 5% intend to find a company and 3% want to succeed in the family business or in an external business (Brisochi et al., 2020). The same trend can be found by examining the international sample, with the significant difference that in both short and medium terms, the incidence of aspiring entrepreneurs is approximately 5% higher than in the Italian sample (Fig. 1).

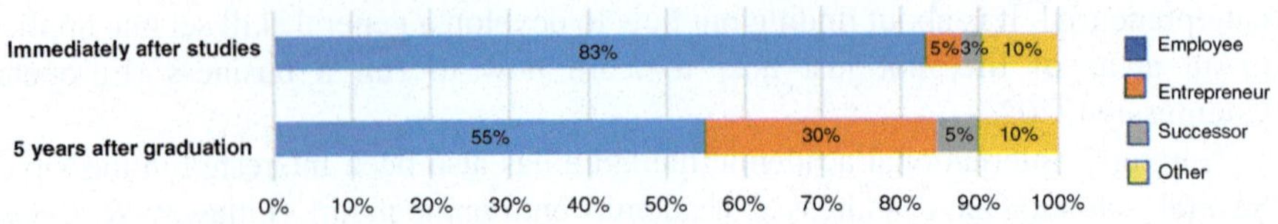

Fig. 1 Career intention in the Italian sample (Source: Parole di Management, 2023)

The idea that an entrepreneurial path does not necessarily represent the first and only career choice is increasingly reflected in the literature. Recent developments in the study of entrepreneurship describe entrepreneurial entry and exit as dynamic processes that can occur throughout an individual's career path (Burton et al., 2016). In fact, it is well known that an entrepreneurial career, from identifying new opportunities to founding and managing a new business, requires a broad versatility and combination of varied skills that are typically greater than the employee, whose activity very often tends to be more specialized (Åstebro & Thompson, 2011).

3 The Role of Universities in the Start-Up Ecosystem

The possibility for universities to become actors in the economic development of a country through the offer of educational training activities and technology transfer and through the provision of services to start-up companies has in recent years grown the interest of many scholars who have concentrated their research on the relationship between these institutions and new entrepreneurship (Petretto, 2007; Fetters et al., 2011). In the United States, for many years, universities have played an important role in the field of entrepreneurship promotion, focusing in particular efforts on the management of intellectual property in promoting the creation of new businesses through both direct and through spin-offs the vehicle of university incubators. For example, Stanford University, more than any other institution, has been considered the engine of the birth and development of the hi-tech economy in California. Before the past decade, Stratford University professors, researchers, and students had founded nearly 3000 companies. Companies such as Sun Microsystem, Cisco Systems, HP (Hewlett Packard), and Google were founded precisely thanks to technological prototypes created by Stratford University (Confindustria, 2009 and Bank of Boston).

A process of evolution oriented in this direction, albeit slowly, is also starting in Italy, where despite a widespread perception of a lack of cooperation between the academic world and the business world, some university institutions are working hard to provide important help to make a more competitive territorial entrepreneurial reality in the face of the new challenges of global innovations and the unstoppable evolution of technologies. Since 2000, the Polytechnic of Turin has collaborated with Motoria for applied research projects; the San Raffaele research park in Milan houses a research center of the pharmaceutical company Schering-Plough; since

2006, the University of Trento has hosted some Microsoft offices; in Naples, since 2017, in the San Giovanni pole, Federico II hosts Apple and Deloitte Academy and Deloitte.

> We can say that the Universities working on education and scientific research aim at dialogue with the institutions spread across the territory and for this they constitute "a possible engine of economic development for the country and sources of diffusion of entrepreneurship in the reference area" (Petretto, 2007 p. 90).

3.1 The Contribution of Universities in Early Entrepreneurship: Resource Network, Opportunity Network, and Legitimation Network

In this subsection, the author highlights a landmark study published in 2001 by Abell, Crouncheley, and Mills on the description of how some networks are able to spur the development of new entrepreneurship. The authors claim that universities, through their role and activities (teaching programs and research projects), are able to activate three categories of networks that enable a potential entrepreneur to place himself in a network and system of relationships that will increase his chances of success:

3.1.1 Legitimation Networks

This category includes the growth of interpersonal ties that provide an ambitious entrepreneur preparing to start a new business credibility.

In particular, the aforementioned legitimation process takes place due to the following:

- The creation of a climate of shared values and principles that favors and legitimizes the spirit of entrepreneurial initiative.
- The creation of a climate of shared values and principles that legitimize entrepreneurial action by increasing self-confidence and the awareness of acting for the well-being of the community with the increase in employment and the development of the local economy.
- The creation of a climate of shared values and principles that increase the feasibility perception and the real possibility of realization of entrepreneurial projects.
- Legitimates and normalizes the psychological needs at the "basis of the entrepreneurial will" such as the need for achievement.

Just think, for example, of the institutions of prizes for the best business ideas by universities.

3.1.2 Opportunity and Resource Network

This category includes the development of relations between individuals who offer start-ups new market opportunities.

The student, professor, or researcher who finds his or her start-up within a university context can meet actors who may have a "complementarity" in entrepreneurial action, reducing the costs and start-up times of the start-up. Just think, for example, of the development of computer algorithms born in the computer labs of the university of information engineering or of the possibility that a new graduate in economics who is starting his start-up to intercept with subjects who usually interact with the teaching and research staff such as venture capitalist or business angel.

Training activities and university teaching could also be an opportunity in these contexts because they offer the potential entrepreneur the opportunity to access managerial and entrepreneurial skills to be used in a business creation process (Fiet, 2001; Vallini & Simoni, 2006).

Finally, it is worth mentioning the possibility that the *start-uppers* linked to the universities must develop new innovations because they are inserted in university technology transfer offices and academic spin-offs. The latter will be explored in the next paragraph (4.4).

Start-uppers who carry out their work in academic settings frequently also have access to coworking facilities, which allows them to both save expenses associated with office and utility fees and to foster contacts with other start-ups and skill-exchange opportunities. This is a factor that, at first appearance, could appear unimportant and is frequently overestimated.

3.1.3 Extracurricular Activators

Activities given by universities, such as clubs, associations, athletic and cultural groups, and campus events, are referred to as extracurricular activities (Petretto, 2007). These activities have different purposes, but they all share the aim of fostering relationships between students, researchers, and professors from all over the world.

This is a networking practice (Mele & Russo-Spena, 2015) that is widespread much more in the United States than in Europe, and certainly in Italy, the commitment in this sense must be increased.

Numerous studies show that students with the greatest spirit of initiative (39%) prefer colleges that provide these sorts of initiatives on campus to serve as proof of the significance of these extracurricular activities (USnews, 2016).

Among these activities, at this point, it is important to focus on associations focused on the specific field of entrepreneurship: entrepreneur clubs and entrepreneur associations.

Entrepreneurial Assuciones are created as organizations with a focus on promoting interdisciplinary cultural activities on certain facets of entrepreneurship that are able to foster the comparison of concepts, studies, and projects among actors connected to universities. The most emblematic example is that of the MIT Alumni Association, a large community that includes the MIT enterprise Forum, the MIT world (network of aspiring university entrepreneurs between the countries of the United States, Japan, Taiwan, England) and the MIT open courseware (courses educational courses made for professors and students by venture capitalists and presidents of investment funds) (mit.edu).

From the above example, it can be assumed that entrepreneurial education contributes to:

- Create and disseminate entrepreneurial culture.
- Facilitate the sharing of ideas and projects.

The strong connection with professors and students from all over the world allows potential entrepreneurs to grasp new insights and follow other best practices.

- Facilitate the transition between idea and execution of entrepreneurial projects.

Very often, these types of associations work in close contact with investment funds, which, by financing university start-ups, have every interest in their success.

- Allow access to skills, expertise and capabilities that are not accessible in other ways.

There will be continuous comparisons with experienced entrepreneurs through the organization of workshops, lectures, and project work supported by large companies.

All this facilitates and promotes access to experiences and competence.

4 University-Based Accelerators and Incubators, a Literature Review

Many academics who have participated in the start-up debate believe that education is crucial to fostering a more flourishing start-up ecosystem (Pittaway & Cope, 2007; Blenker et al., 2013; Landström & Harirchi, 2019). Indeed, both scholars who choose to focus on resources (e.g., Cukier & Kon, 2018) and authors who attribute significance to many elements agree that knowledge is a crucial foundation of a start-up ecosystem (Frederiksen & Brem, 2017). According to several studies (Petretto, 2008; Tripathi et al., 2018), entrepreneurs encounter a few harder-than-normal difficulties and impediments in places where there is a lack of education. The lack of courses in developing soft skills in the school curriculum is one factor contributing to this deficiency (Tripathi et al., 2018). Since the debate over the triple helix began, this literary field has viewed universities as enabling entrepreneurship through a concentration on teaching (Etzkowitz & Leydesdorff, 2000). In fact, the university plays a role in bridging government and business to create an environment that is conducive to innovation. The Local Innovative System serves a similar purpose by encouraging reciprocal learning processes in a region to encourage new businesses and innovation results. Universities, along with other players from the industrial and political spheres, are part of this initiative (Ferretti & Parmentola, 2015; Ventura et al., 2019). Due to the benefits of mixing various knowledge and innovation modes, the argument over helix models has evolved to the point where an ecosystem is now thought of as a helix (Carayannis et al., 2018). One of the first contributions on UBAs framed them—as well as university-based incubators—as entities supporting "entrepreneurial teams during the early stage" (Stayton & Mangematin, 2016); a restrictive approach to UBAs was preferred by Breznitz and Zhang (2019), who described them as an organization supporting firms' growth with specific reference to "graduates' development as entrepreneurs" (p. 868). Ismail (2020), in a similar vein, noted the services provided to students who were interested in a career as entrepreneurs and qualified to gain from the provision of "the unique viewpoint of combining business and entrepreneurial theory and practice" (p. 3). UBAs are part of a regional entrepreneurial ecosystem, in addition to often being connected to time-limited programs (Mansoori et al., 2019).

When UBAs showed their extensive skills and thrived in diverse situations, the discussion over the role of universities in entrepreneurship and from an ecosystem-oriented viewpoint grew even more heated (Stayton & Mangematin, 2019).

UBAs are one of the most recent developments in this area of research, although there have not been many contributions that specifically address them. To better understand the role of these accelerators, Table 2 summarizes the aforementioned themes from the three perspectives on the start-up ecosystem literature. This review on UBAs views actors, geographic contexts, and resources as the three main drivers shaping a start-up ecosystem and the support it can provide for the start-up's growth. In the next subsections, which are each devoted to a distinct viewpoint on start-ups and applied to UBAs, the functions of UBAs will be further discussed.

4.1 The Distinctive Characteristics of UBI (University Business Incubator)

The two most popular types of incubators and accelerators for start-up businesses have emerged, namely, traditional business incubators, which are typically private or even public with the participation of venture funds, and UBI, a university business incubator. This classification of incubators and accelerators for start-up companies was first proposed in the previous chapter. The two most popular types of incubators differ significantly from one another, making university incubators the only ones of their sort. First, in the case of traditional BICs, as we have seen above, start-up companies or innovative business projects are selected by the competent incubator from a series of proposals that derive from the external environment, while in the case of UBI, the projects of companies are mostly derived from internal academic research. This is a significant distinction between BIC and UBI since, at least during

Table 2 The three viewpoints on the responsibilities of accelerators in the start-up ecosystem literature

Perspectives from start-ups literature	Key topic	Accelerators' functions, including those of UBAs	Main references
Actors	Dynamicity, openness, mechanisms for renewal, relationships between actors, and spillovers	UBA directors may catalyze procedures depending on their expertise in technology transfers and their background. UBAs are crucial agents favoring start-up ecosystem expansion and ongoing reshaping.	Breznitz and Zhang (2019); Condom-Vilà (2020); Hernández & González (2016); Krajcik & Formanek (2015); Mansoori et al. (2019); Stayton and Mangematin (2016).
Geographical context	Local assistance, area economics, social and cultural context, information environment, and other factors	UBAs enable the correct and effective coordination of local players to facilitate the expansion of start-ups. UBAs coordinate local actors, therefore influencing the environment in which entrepreneurs may flourish.	Audretsch & Belitski (2017); Bernhofer & Han (2014); Cukier et al. (2016); Ismail 2020; Spigel (2015).
Resources	Knowledge, risk capital, permeability, integration and fluidity, learning, experience, and mentorship	UBAs assist start-ups by making direct investments and luring in a variety of important resources. Start-ups are impacted by several factors, including the financial resources, expertise, timing, and structures of UBAs.	Baloutsos et al. (2020); Hemmert et al. (2016); Malecki (2018); Stayton and Mangematin (2016); Ventura et al. (2019);

the incubation phase, the start-ups of the latter will face less competition from the start-up business market than the BICs. Given that the development of new business initiatives necessitates a transfer of technology and skills to the external market, this does not imply that start-ups with a university background will not have to deal with the external market.

There are also more aspects of the UBI offer that are often associated with universities. Other aspects of the UBI offer that are characteristic of university incubator operations include:

- The accessibility of networks, logistics, and secretarial services; fundamental support for company development; and the availability of places.

- Specialized services for the academic setting, such as advice for professors, use of libraries, labs, and scientific infrastructures, market research initiatives, and technology transfer initiatives.
- A UBI gives repute, one of the main factors among those that define university incubation activities, in addition to the accessibility of services and abilities of the academic environment. A company that is created in an incubator connected to a reputable institution that is well known and respected in the industry would undoubtedly benefit from this, including easier access to the university's privileged contacts, quicker market acceptance, and building a good reputation with investors.

5 Academic Spin-Offs

The term spin-off, in general, refers to new companies born using resources (financing, know-how, technologies, human resources, relationships, etc.) made available by a main organization such as large companies, research centers, and universities (Sorrentino et al., 2012; Kroll & Liefner, 2008).

As far as university spin-offs are concerned, it must be said that in recent years, they have particularly increased as a phenomenon given the expansion in the objectives of university missions. Therefore, the first mission (teaching for student) and the second mission (research activity) are accompanied by a third university mission, which means that the university must also "exploit economically" the contributions of the studies and research carried out indoors (Van Looy et al., 2011). The third university mission concerns a real "opening towards the socioeconomic context through the enhancement and transfer of knowledge" (Anvur, 2002). University spin-offs are companies and business projects that arise from the results of university research in each sector. With reference to academic spin-offs, therefore, the main objective is to pursue the so-called "conversion" process, the transformation of a university research result or a specific technology developed at the university into an entrepreneurial project. Therefore, when the reference organization is a university and the subjects that come together to give life to a business are researchers, professors, students, or even administrative staff to practice or commercially exploit the results of their research, in this case, we can speak of academic spin-offs (Piccarozzi, 2013). Academic spin-offs, therefore, play the role of fostering technology transfer processes by helping to bridge the gap between the point where university research ends and the point where market interest begins (Cesaroni et al., 2005).

Observing the trend in the United States, we note that the start-ups born from academic spin-offs are on average 2000 per year (Surveys AUTM data).

The phenomenon in Italy, although growing, is still at an early stage, and only in the 2000s did it begin to grow considerably (Fig. 2).

In 2021, there will be 1752 active spin-offs of public research in Italy (Spin-off Italia, 2021).

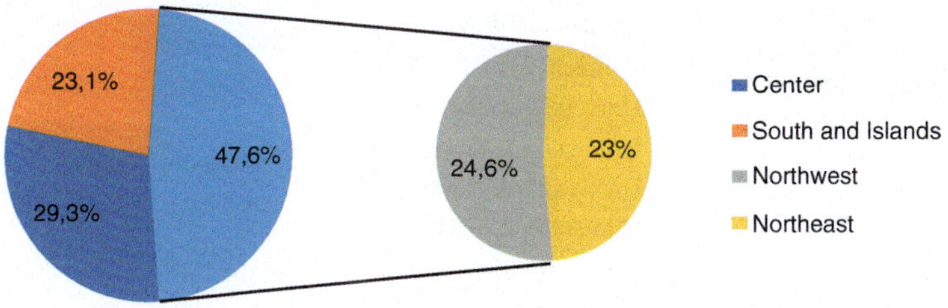

Fig. 2 Coccorullo and Boffo reworking (2018) on the distribution in Italy of academic spin-offs

Another interesting fact for the purposes of a quantitative analysis of the phenomenon in question is that relating to the geographical location of the spin-offs. In particular, it is evident that the initially most active regions from the point of view of the creation of research spin-offs have maintained a high level of companies for each year: the phenomenon is evidently concentrated in the northern regions where moreover, 47.6% of the spin-offs are located, despite being on the increase in the Center (29.3%), while the remaining 23.1% is distributed between the South and the Islands. The latter are, also in this field, the least active territories due to the very serious economic difficulties they traditionally experience, which were heavily aggravated by the 2008 crisis. Table 3 shows the spin-offs currently active in the main Italian universities. The number of active spin-offs reported in the table for each university should be interpreted in an indicative way. In fact, some universities only indicate the number of spin-offs already incorporated on their institutional websites. Others instead make a distinction between those already qualified and incorporated and those pending. Still others have spin-offs in both states on the same list (Table 3).

Finally, another interesting aspect is that of the main sectors in which academic spin-offs are widespread. Specifically, the sector that seems to incorporate the largest number of companies (23.9%) is that of ICT (Information and Communications Technology) (see graph 5), immediately followed by services for innovation (22.9%). Fewer spin-offs concern the energy and environment sectors (16.3%) and life sciences (15.6%), and very few concern biomedical ones (7.2%), electronics (5.5%), and industrial automation (3.6%) (Netval, 2022). According to the Netval report, there will be 1384 university spin-offs in 2022, and their duration will reach 8 years with a survival rate of 86%.

Table 3 Number of spin-offs shown on the institutional websites of the main Italian public universities Author's elaboration (2023)

Politecnico di Milano	63
Politecnico di Torino	74
Università di Padova	62
Università la Sapienza di Roma	53
Università di Bologna	54
Università di Pisa	32
Università di Palermo	32
Università Federico II di Napoli	91
Università degli Studi di Firenze	46
Università di Torino	53
Università di Perugia	44
Università di Bari Aldo Moro	40
Università Tor Vergata di Roma	21
Università di Pavia	22
Politecnico delle Marche	56
Università di Genova	40
Università di Salerno	18
Università della Calabria	47
Università di Parma	18
Università di Cagliari	22
Università di Verona	30
Università di Ferrara	12
Università di Messina	17
Università di Modena e Reggio Emilia	20
Università di Catania	25
Università di Venezia	14

References

Antonaci, A., Bellotti, F., Berta, R., Dagnino, F. M., De Gloria, A., Lavagnino, E., & Ott, M. (2014). Educazione all'imprenditorialità: Spunti di riflessione. *Italian Journal of Educational Technology, 22*(2), 68–73.

Anvur. (2002). Official site of the Italian National Agency for the Evaluation of the University and Research System. www.anvur

Åstebro, T., & Thompson, P. (2011). Entrepreneurs, jacks of all trades or hobos? *Research Policy, 40*(5), 637–649.

Audretsch, D. B., & Belitski, M. (2017). Entrepreneurial ecosystems in cities: Establishing the framework conditions. *The Journal of Technology Transfer, 42*, 1030–1051.

Bala Subrahmanya, M. H. (2017). How did Bangalore emerge as a global hub of tech start-ups in India? Entrepreneurial ecosystem—Evolution, structure, and role. *Journal of Developmental Entrepreneurship, 22*(01), 1750006.

Baloutsos, S., Karagiannaki, A., & Mourtos, I. (2020). Business Model Generation for Industry 4.0: A "Lean Startup" approach. *The International Technology Management Review, 9*(1), 34–45.

Bernhofer, L., & Han, Z. (2014). Contextual factors and their effects on future entrepreneurs in China: A comparative study of entrepreneurial intentions. *International Journal of Technology Management, 65*(1–4), 125–150.

Blenker, P., Dreisler, P., Faergemann, H. M., & Kjeldsen, J. (2013). A framework for developing entrepreneurship education in a university context. *International Journal of Entrepreneurship and Small Business, 5*(1), 45–63.

Breznitz, S. M., & Zhang, Q. (2019). Fostering the growth of student start-ups from university accelerators: An entrepreneurial ecosystem perspective. *Industrial and Corporate Change, 28*(4), 855–873.

Brisochi M.S., Hahn D., Minola T., (2020). Imprenditrialità studentesca, un fenomeno in forte crescita,. Parole di Management.

Burton, M. D., Sørensen, J. B., & Dobrev, S. D. (2016). A careers perspective on entrepreneurship. *Entrepreneurship Theory and Practice, 40*(2), 237–247.

Carayannis, E. G., Grigoroudis, E., Campbell, D. F., Meissner, D., & Stamati, D. (2018). The ecosystem as helix: An exploratory theory-building study of regional co-operative entrepreneurial ecosystems as Quadruple/Quintuple Helix Innovation Models. *R&D Management, 48*(1), 148–162.

Cesaroni, F., Di Minin, A., & Piccaluga, A. (2005). Exploration and exploitation strategies in industrial R&D.

Condom-Vilà, P. (2020). *Ciencia, tecnología y startups*. Edicions Universitat Barcelona.

Consolini, M., Di Saverio, M., Loasses, C., & Richini, P. (2013). *Indicazioni per la programmazione e la realizzazione di iniziative per l'educazione all'imprenditorialità.*

Cukier, D., & Kon, F. (2018). A maturity model for software start-up ecosystems. *Journal of Innovation and Entrepreneurship, 7*(1), 14.

Cukier, D., Kon, F., & Lyons, T. S. (2016, June). Software startup ecosystems evolution: The New York City case study. In *2016 International Conference on Engineering, Technology and Innovation/IEEE lnternational Technology Management Conference (ICE/ITMC)* (pp. 1–8). IEEE.

Etzkowitz, H., & Leydesdorff, L. (2000). The dynamics of innovation: From National Systems and "Mode 2" to a Triple Helix of university–industry–government relations. *Research Policy, 29*(2), 109–123.

European Commission. (2022). Official site of European Commission. www.commission.europa.eu

Frederiksen, D. L., & Brem, A. (2017). How do entrepreneurs think they create value? A scientific reflection of Eric Ries' Lean Start-up approach. *International Entrepreneurship and Management Journal, 13*, 169–189.

Ferretti, M., & Parmentola, A. (2015). *The creation of local innovation systems in emerging countries: The role of governments, firms and universities*. Springer.

Fetters, M., Patricia, G., & Rice, M. P. (2011). *The development of university-based entrepreneurship ecosystems*. Global Practices.

Fiet, J. O. (2001). The theoretical side of teaching entrepreneurship. *Journal of Business Venturing, 16*(1), 1–24.

Fraiberg, S. (2017). Start-up nation: Studying transnational entrepreneurial practices in Israel's start-up ecosystem. *Journal of Business and Technical Communication, 31*(3), 350–388.

Gupta, R. K. (2023). Does university entrepreneurial ecosystem and entrepreneurship education affect the students' entrepreneurial intention/start-up intention? In *Industry 4.0 and advanced manufacturing* (pp. 355–365). Springer.

Hemmert, M., Kim, D., Kim, J., & Cho, B. (2016). Building the supplier's trust: Role of institutional forces and buyer firm practices. *International Journal of Production Economics, 180*, 25–37.

Hernández, C., & González, D. (2016). Study of the start-up ecosystem in Lima, Peru: Collective case study. *Latin American Business Review, 17*(2), 115–137.

Ismail, A. (2020). Building a university-centered Entrepreneurship Ecosystem: A Case study of the American university in Cairo. *Entrepreneurship and Innovation in Egypt*, 147–161.

Joshi, K., & Satyanarayana, K. (2014). What ecosystem factors impact the growth of high-tech start-ups in India? *Asian Journal of Innovation and Policy, 3*(2), 216–244.

Krajcik, V., & Formanek, I. (2015). Regional startup ecosystem. *European Business & Management, 1*(2), 14–18.

Kroll, H., & Liefner, I. (2008). Spin-off enterprises as a means of technology commercialization in a transforming economy. *Technovation, 28*(5), 298–313.

Landström, H., & Harirchi, G. (2019). "That's interesting!" in entrepreneurship research. *Journal of Small Business Management, 57*(sup2), 507–529.

Malecki, E. J. (2018). Entrepreneurship and entrepreneurial ecosystems. *Geography Compass, 12* (3), e12359.

Mansoori, Y., Karlsson, T., & Lundqvist, M. (2019). The influence of the lean start-up methodology on entrepreneur-coach relationships in the context of a start-up accelerator. *Technovation, 84*, 37–47.

Mele, C., & Russo-Spena, T. (2015). Innomediary agency and practices in shaping market innovation. *Industrial Marketing Management, 44*, 42–53.

Petretto, L. (2007). *Università nello start up di impresa, ruoli e relazioni critiche* (Imprenditore ed.). Firenze University Press.

Petretto, L. (2008). Il rapporto tra Università ed. early entrepreneurship: le opportunità per gli imprenditori nei processi di start-up. *Il rapporto tra Università ed early entrepreneurship*, 1000–1054.

Pittaway, L., & Cope, J. (2007). Entrepreneurship education: A systematic review of the evidence. *International Small Business Journal, 25*(5), 479–510.

Sawhney, M. (2002). Do not just relate-Collaborate. *Mitsloan Management Review, 43*(3), 96.

Smilor, R. W., & Gibson, D. V. (1991). Accelerating technology transfer in R&D consortia. *Research-Technology Management, 34*(1), 44–49.

Sorrentino, M., Matricano, D., Guadalupi, L., Tutore, V., & Andreottola, F., (2012). "*The Creation of Academic Spin-offs: Evidences from Italy*," DSI Essays Series, DSI - Dipartimento di Studi sull'Impresa, vol. 27.

Stayton, J., & Mangematin, V. (2016). Start-up time, innovation and organizational emergence: A study of USA-based international technology ventures. *Journal of International Entrepreneurship, 14*(3), 373–409.

Stayton, J., & Mangematin, V. (2019). Seed accelerators and the speed of new venture creation. *The Journal of Technology Transfer, 44*(4), 1163–1187.

Piccarozzi, M. (2013). An innovation transfer's network: University spin-offs, venture capital and public funds. In *Organizational change and information systems* (pp. 275–283). Springer.

Tripathi, V., Singh, A. P., & Roy, R. (2018). Effect of economic growth initiatives on regional economies: A study in the Indian context. *International Journal of Entrepreneurship and Innovation Management, 22*(3), 286–297.

Usnews. (2016). High circulation Washington magazine. www.usnews.com

Vallini, C., & Simoni, C. (2006). *Higer Education and Entrepreneurial vocation and capabilities*. Firenze University Press.

Van Looy, B., Landoni, P., & Van Pottelsbreghe, B. (2011). Entrepreneurial Effectiveness of European University. *Research Policy, 40*, 553.

Vanevenhoven, J. (2013). Advances and challenges in entrepreneurship education. *Journal of Small Business Management, 51*(3), 466–470.

Vanhaverbeke, W., & Cloodt, M. (2014). Theories of the firm and open innovation. In *New frontiers in open innovation* (p. 256).

Ventura, R. Quero, M.J. & Díaz-Méndez, M. (2019). *The role of institutions in achieving radical innovation, Marketing Intelligence & Planning.*

Wilson, K. E. (2008). Entrepreneurship education in Europe. *Entrepreneurship and higher education*.

Access to New Technologies as a Lever for Start-Up Scalability

1 Introduction

Increasingly, in recent years, new technologies have been implemented not only by large companies but also by new start-up companies (Agrawal et al., 2017). Accessibility to technologies in start-up ecosystems is not a negligible aspect. The issues of digital transformation and new technologies are treated as a lever for the main objectives of start-ups, such as scalability and replicability. A focus on the development and use of artificial intelligence, much exploited, in the context of start-up ecosystems, is addressed in detail.

The explanation for the diffusion of the phenomenon of start-up companies promoting new technologies lies in the fact that it is not easy to create new technological solutions in organizations that are too large. At the same time, it is impossible to create new technologies alone, and the "one men band" in business creation does not work. The right compromise would be small creative organizations where the limited size "leaves room for better thinking" (Thiel, 2014). Therefore, to forge the new technologies of the future, according to Thiel (2014), the change must not take place in a "horizontal" sense in terms of global production volume but must take place in a "vertical" sense, "from zero to one." The act of creation is unique, as is the moment in which it takes place. The result of the latter is something that only happens once, and for this reason, it must be pursued and preserved at all costs to achieve true innovation.

The sectors in which most of the so-called "unicorn" start-ups are present, i.e., those that exceed a value of 2 billion dollars, are emblematic and are represented in Fig. 1 .

F. Greco, *Startup Ecosystems*, Studies on Entrepreneurship, Structural Change and Industrial Dynamics, https://doi.org/10.1007/978-3-031-34414-5_5

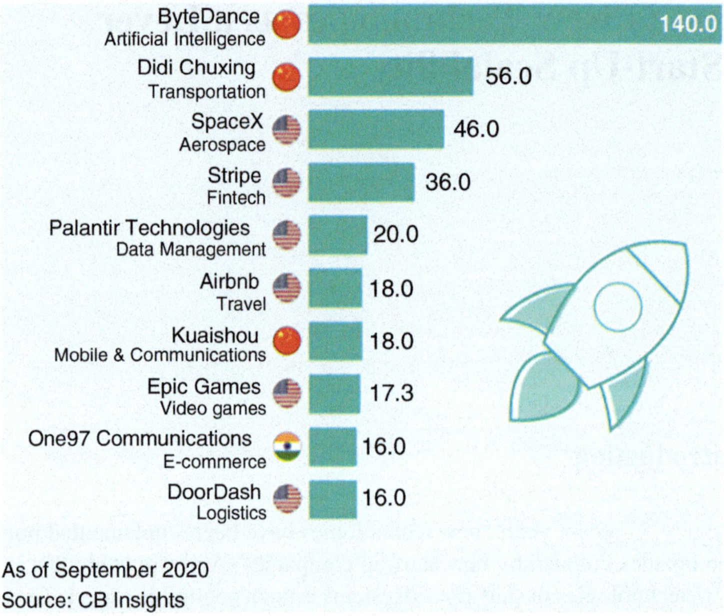

Fig. 1 The 10 sectors in which the 10 "unicorn" start-ups in the world are present

2 Start-Up and Digital Transformation

For all firms, digital transformation is essential. People typically associate digital transformation with a certain degree of technology since it solely refers to the technical expenditures that businesses make. This confusion results from the outdated definition of digital transformation, which reads: "the use of new digital technologies, such as social media, mobile, analytics, or embedded devices to enable major business improvements, like enhancing customer experience, streamlining operations, or creating new business models" (Fitzgerald et al., 2013) or "a process that involves the proliferation of the Internet in both demand and supply sector" (Bounfour, 2016). Therefore, digital transformation of course means investments in technology, implementation, practice, and automation of the whole company; however, this is not the only meaning: authors such as Stolterman and Fors gave the following definition: "the changes that digital technology causes or influences in all aspects in human life" (Stolterman & Fors, 2004). According to Boulton (2018), the term "digital transformation" has become widely used in business media to describe the disruptive or transformational effects of digital technologies on businesses (new business models, new types of products/services, and new types of customer experiences). However, digital transformation affects customers, activities, processes, business models, and technology, and it has much to do with strategy. The phenomena include spending money on new hardware and software, but it also necessitates a mental shift among the populace and the development of a potent organizationally backed company-level strategy.

Traditional business paradigms are changing significantly as a result of digital transformation: new organizational roles are emerging, a new entrepreneurial culture is becoming more necessary, and the reference ecosystem for innovation is changing due to the entry of new players such as start-up companies and tools such as artificial intelligence (AI). Digital maturity is essential and a must. It is essential for a business to successfully implement a digital transformation, and start-up enterprises may perform substantially better thanks to AI as a science that can create complicated systems.

Start-ups, digital transformation companies, and AI have complementary ideas: digital disruptors and creative start-ups are reshaping traditional companies by using current procedures, goods, services, and content while utilizing new technology, particularly artificial intelligence.

According to a 2019 study by the British venture capital firm MMC Venture, the landscape for start-up entrepreneurs has altered, and the dynamics of AI entrepreneurship in Europe are developing. The 1600 AI companies in Europe have grown up in 2019, disrupting new sectors and navigating new chances and difficulties. Suffice it to say that "in 2013, just 1 out of 50 new start-ups embraced AI and in 2019, 1 in 12 put AI at the heart of their value proposition, so the percentage of European medium and large companies employing artificial intelligence technologies has gone from 4% to 12%. The group is led by the United Kingdom, with almost 479 start-ups that take advantage of AI technologies, more than double that of France, which follows with 217 companies, and Germany, third at 196. In eighth position there is Italy, with 66 highly technological start-ups" (MMC Venture, 2019). As of 2022, 15 k innovative start-ups in Italy have increased employment by 6% per half year, with over 75,000 shareholders. Two million yuan in fundraising and over 60,000 employees have been reached, sufficing to say that at the end of September 2022, approximately 3 k innovative start-ups started thanks to a digital and free establishment method (Sole24Ore, 2019). A year of growth for Italian Innovative Start-ups maybe 2020. It is now possible to use the Fondo Nazionale Innovazione (FNI). To better match the interests of Italian investors and entrepreneurs with the shared objective of economic growth, the government may be able to participate through venture capital operations in key enterprises and start-ups. This would provide a wonderful chance to produce new resources (MISE, 2021). The literature on start-ups and artificial intelligence is rather sparse, and there is still little scientific evidence on the subject, but the conditions are promising and rather than positive. Therefore, the next chapter will propose a review on start-ups and artificial intelligence (initiated by the author during his studies for his PhD thesis) with the aim of laying the foundations for research based on highlighting the link between these two themes.

Before dealing with the specific chapter concerning the use of AI by start-ups, an in-depth analysis is proposed concerning the principles of scalability and replicability. These are directly connected, as we will see, to the accessibility and use of new technologies by Italian start-up companies.

2.1 New Technologies and the Concept of Start-Up Scalability and Start-Up Replicability

As we have already defined in the chapter dedicated to entrepreneurship, scalability, and replicability are terms and concepts that are always associated with a start-up. Two are concepts of extreme importance in terms of evaluating potential, to the point of being considered to become the borderline between a "normal" business project and a real innovative start-up.

The adjective "scalable" and thus the term "Scalability" means a business that can increase its size—and therefore its customers and its volume—even exponentially without the use of proportional resources (Nielsen & Lund, 2018). The start-up, to be such, must therefore be able to take advantage of the economies of scale and thus generate costs that they grow in a manner not proportional to revenue growth.

In particular, the concept of "Scalability" for obvious reasons is particularly connected to that of new technologies. The latter are the determining factors for obtaining a scalable business model.

As a main example, just think of the logistics algorithms that have made it possible to optimize the entire delivery process of delivery companies.

In the information and communication technologies sector, scalability is represented by the ability of a system, network, or process to flexibly and dynamically manage an increase in workload or the addition of new features. The intrinsic limits are therefore linked to the software and hardware architecture of the system itself (Priestley, 2018).

Replicable refers to the ability of your product, service, or business to be replicated and sold, and delivered consistently and reliably, to serve (theoretically) infinite customers the exact same service or product, to the exact same standard, every time. Therefore, by replicable start-up, we mean an innovative company that has a business model that can be repeated in different places and in different periods without the need for major adjustments, thus introducing new appropriate solutions in different communities (Maiolini & Giudici, 2019).

> ...Some examples of replicable products would be nearly anything that comes off a high-volume production line (e.g. iPhones), McDonald's Cheeseburgers (mostly), Xero's accounting app, subscription TV....
>
> .... Examples of nonreplicable products include custom motor bikes, architecturally designed homes, Oscar winning movies, and advertising campaigns. If your product or service requires new thinking or relies on the expertise of particular individuals each time it is delivered, it's not replicable.....
>
> (nzentrepreneur, 2017).

In the literature, the debate is undoubtedly open to understanding whether it is the creations of the most "disruptive" businesses that give life to scalable and innovative business models in a technological sense or if, conversely, the latter is precisely the result of high-value technological implementations. Many scholars have investigated this issue (Kostoff & Boylan, 2004; Bower & Clayton, 1995; Chesbrough (2003).

The emerging phenomenon of scale-ups is certainly very connected to the theme of scalability and to that of technology, which are types of start-ups that reach higher stages of development:

Alberto Onetti (2014), of the Mind the Bridge Foundation, asserts, "*Your start-up becomes a scaleup after it has validated its business model, solved the challenges facing the start-up, and is therefore ready for growth., an exponential growth.*"

Additionally, Onetti, in a comment made to Start-up business (2017), had given this definition of scale-up:

> "Scaleups are start-ups that have reached a" "critical mass" "and are ready to become relevant taxpayers for the economy (both in terms of revenue generation and the jobs they offer to people). There are different types of "critical mass" for different types of business."

We define this transition from start-up to scale up with the aphorism "crossing the chasm of growth", inspired by the definition of Geoffrey Moore (2016) in his book "Crossing the Chasm" dedicated to scaleups.

3 "Accessibility" to New Technologies in Italy

Big Data, Artificial Intelligence, and Machine Learning are just a few of the technological developments that technology companies hope to use to change a variety of industries, including health, Fintech, Biotech, Edtech start-ups, and Food. The use of new technologies is crucial for achieving the so-called "Scalability" and "Replicability" objectives of start-ups.

There are several theoretical contributions that describe the commitment of accelerators and incubators of start-up companies to favor and support not so much the development of new technologies at the service of start-ups but more to the accessibility of the latter for start-ups (Aernoudt, 2004; Bruneel et al., 2012; Petretto, 2007).

A particular connection between new technologies and Scalability and Replicability are the concepts of Horizontal Scalability, Vertical Scalability, and Virtualization (Zaki & Hussein, 2019).

Horizontal scaling consists of adding hardware components to meet demand. For example, it involves equipping multiple servers (even temporarily) to cope with increased flows and load balancing.

Vertical scalability means adding components to existing machines. Let us take the example of servers, which can benefit from additional resources (processor, memory, etc.) which increase their performance.

Vertical scaling, unlike horizontal scaling, is more limited. In fact, while it is possible to extend your IT park indefinitely (provided you have the means, of course), the capabilities of a single server are reduced.

Virtualization is the possibility of grouping the various IT resources (servers, operating systems, software, etc.) of the company on a single machine. This process brings much more flexibility, both in terms of horizontal and vertical scaling.

Among the necessary requirements established by the MISE to obtain the appointment of "certified incubator," a start-up support organization must, in fact, have "adequate technological equipment for the activity of innovative start-ups, such as ultrabroadband access systems to the network internet, hardware machinery, tests or necessary technological prototypes" (MISE, 2021).

In Italy, among the measures that the MISE promotes for the development of new innovative technologies and above all for greater accessibility by all start-up companies and small businesses to the latter, it is worth mentioning that of "Voucher for digitization."

That is, a facilitating measure for micro, small, and medium-sized enterprises that provides for a contribution, through the granting of a "voucher," for an amount not exceeding 10,000 euros, aimed at the adoption of digitization interventions of business processes and technological modernization.

The implementing discipline of the measure was adopted with the interministerial decree of September 23, 2014.

The voucher can be used to purchase software, hardware, and/or specialist services that allow you to:

- Improve business efficiency.
- Modernize the organization of work, using technological tools and forms of work flexibility, including teleworking.
- Develop e-commerce solutions.
- Benefit from broadband and ultrabroadband connectivity or Internet connection through satellite technology.
- Carry out qualified training of personnel in the ICT field (MISE, 2020).

There are several other measures promoted by the MISE to encourage and support the development and accessibility of start-ups to new technologies. In this way, we try to make the fabric of start-up companies more attractive to the venture capital market, to facilitate and encourage open innovation processes, and to increase the competitiveness of Italian companies in the international context.

4 Artificial Intelligence-Based Start-Ups: Insight and Outlooks in Italy

As we have noted from the ranking of "unicorn" start-ups in the world, one of the most widespread new technologies used to support almost all innovative industrial sectors is undoubtedly that of artificial intelligence (Fig. 1).

The literature on the subject of the relationship between start-up businesses and artificial intelligence has received very little attention. There is currently a dearth of scientific data supporting the merging of AI with start-ups. The thesis that artificial intelligence is a key, practical, and successful engine for an innovative start-up company is increased by several positive and promising contributions, such as the case studies examined. However, as we can see, the professional and educational context in Italy needs to be improved. History teaches us that the major technological firms that are promoting artificial intelligence now, such as Apple, Google, and Amazon, were start-ups when they first appeared. The earliest goods that hit the market already showed a propensity toward using artificial intelligence systems in the future.

Numerous reactions are being sparked by the surge in interest in AI, ranging from enthusiasm about how start-up organizations' capabilities may rise swiftly (Agrawal et al., 2017) leading to an increase in scale-ups. Furthermore, there is a genuine danger that artificial intelligence may develop into a straightforward formula for raising more money. Start-ups that utilize the concept "Ai" receive on average 15–50% more investment than those that are simply, and perhaps more honestly, merely technologically oriented, according to Kelnar (2019), head of research at MMC Ventures.

The risk of artificial intelligence is two-dimensional and opens a double scenario for the Italian start-up environment. The Italian markets may not yet be developed from a commercial standpoint. Instead, from a technological standpoint, one of the major commercial obstacles faced by European and particularly Italian start-uppers is the chance of failure in scientific research. As a result, AI companies should be viewed as business labs that base their trials on recent algorithmic research—"a concept that is not readily captured by typical due diligence scans," according to Global Consulting Roland Berger. Consequently, the emphasis should not be on a quick return on investment and research and development outcomes. Setting larger incentives for risk and return should be essential since doing so will increase the likelihood of acquiring start-ups and increase the profitability of exits.

The lack of integrated training capable of giving businesses, professionals, and young people the tools necessary to better face the jobs of the nearest future is one of the main reasons Italy is at the bottom of the ranking regarding AI implementation when compared to the United States context and other European countries. The culture of taking risks, which is considered a resource for sharing with greater vigor and experimentation, is not encouraged by the Italian educational system and the conventional workplace future.

By creating and celebrating success stories that highlight our talents, Italian successful start-ups and successful companies can be encouraged to use corporate risk capital to invest in emerging technologies. Even foreign digital entrepreneurs may find Italy to be the ideal location where innovation and esthetic appreciation can coexist everywhere (Marinoni & Voorheis, 2019). In this approach, Italy may be able to draw investment and gradually solidify a vocation for the type of business that will be centered on the emergence and expansion of successful start-ups that employ artificial intelligence. To maximize the benefits of AI, operations must be restructured. This should be done in conjunction with a revival of the Italian educational system. Start-ups must first identify and outline an operational area that may be improved before they can do this.

4.1 Case Studies of Italian Start-Ups that Exploit Artificial Intelligence

The analysis of several case studies of Italian AI-based start-ups allows classification into three groups based on the target audience of the activity and the main effect they currently deliver. For this reason, the three groups are "Data Analysis for Market," "Data Analysis for Marketing," and "Tools." All cases forming the first two groups offer B2B services, while the "Tools" group hosts B2C or B2B solutions.

The three preselected start-ups for each identified category are shown Table 1.

4.1.1 Travel Appeal

The largest database in the prospective tourist sector is created by Travel Appeal, which gathers information from more than 500 sources. The analysis of these data produces a few algorithms, which in turn produce information in the form of visuals, maps, and trends. The primary goal of the anticipated information is to synthesize patterns and forecast pricing, the number of visitors who will visit a location, and anticipated earnings for hospitality businesses. With this product, the company asserts that it will be possible to boost businesses' revenue by up to 25%, create more jobs, and favor more direct bookings by up to 7%, enabling stronger profit margins for businesses. Nearly 3000 companies have signed up for this service as of right now, and some of them have even used chatbots to develop fresh travel suggestions for visitors (Source: Start-upitalia.it, 2020).

4.1.2 Cynny

Cynny developed an artificial intelligence platform that can identify a user's gender, age, and emotions. The website provides a program called MorphCast that analyses facial expressions and may modify marketing materials according to users' emotions, gender, age, and possibly additional characteristics in the future. The program may be integrated into other marketing tools that a company already uses and is run on a distant server. Furthermore, approximately 95% of people can correctly identify gender and emotions. Since huge data consumption and software features ensure data protection, Cynny has previously dealt with issues relating to privacy and data management (Source: Crowdfundme.it, 2022).

Table 1 Cases of Italian start-ups that exploit artificial intelligence

Name of start-up	Industry	Category	Market
Travel Appeal	Tourism	Data analysis for market	B2B
Cynny	Video	Data analysis for marketing'	B2B
Musixmatch	Music	"Tools"	B2B-B2C

4.1.3 Musixmatch

Musixmatch gathers, disseminates, and examines song lyrics from all around the world. The company's mission is to create the largest global dataset of lyrics. The services are geared toward both end users and other machine learning-using businesses. In the first scenario, users can search for song lyrics, while businesses using this service can make recommendations and further analyze lyrics in search of emotions, reactions, and relationships between songs (Source: Start-upitalia.it, 2022).

The case studies we analyzed helped us grasp some more meanings about what artificial intelligence can offer to start-ups. Artificial intelligence may be viewed as a launching pad for new goods, services, and methods of operation, which considerably stimulates commercial innovation. In effect, fresh investments in start-ups may be accompanied by artificial intelligence as a carrier of new chances to be infused in new enterprises and generating the potential to revolutionize markets and firms' operations. This is because of the good effects new technologies have on the Italian and global context.

5 Start-Up and Big Data Analytics. International Outlook

Start-ups are also among the main players in the big data scenario. The latter plays an important role as a true source of innovation. Monitoring the performance of the analytics start-up ecosystem at an international level can mean intercepting new business models that can make a difference from a competitive point of view and characterize the market in the years to come.

Both scholars and practitioners have devoted attention to the phenomenon. One of the first studies, among the best known, observed whether the use of big data by large companies could be adopted, with due care, also by start-up companies (Davenport & Dyché, 2013). Seggie et al. (2017), a few years later, provide a study of the integrated process for learning business innovation through the combination of the lean start-up methodology with big data. They assert that the velocity of big data may trigger confirmation bias, communication problems, and illusions of control and that the lean start-up approach (Ries, 2011) may be able to resolve these issues.

Behl et al. (2019) propose a more advanced and complex study. They worked to develop an interpretive structural model to serve as a framework for the efficient implementation of big data analytics (BDA). This framework was then tested by using a case study, and the findings showed that the framework's foundation—access to relevant data—would serve as the largest enabler of adoption, while the organization views workers' technical skill sets (on BDA) as the most crucial enabler.

Moving attention toward a more operational analysis, reference can be made to the fact that thanks to the data from the Digital Innovation observatories of *Politecnico di Milano* (Ciani, 2022), it is possible to identify 721 start-up companies operating in the Big Data Analytics market. Through this sorting, the surveyed start-ups operating in the Big Data market can be organized into four macro areas, for each of which subcategories have been identified.

5.1 Data Enricher

Data Enricher start-ups offer solutions that facilitate the exchange and sale of data. They represent 12% of start-ups dedicated to big data and are divided into two subcategories:

Data Provider: Platforms that make available data regarding certain phenomena (such as the transaction of different sectors) and, in some cases, also the related insights.

Data Marketplace: Solutions aimed at facilitating the provision and acquisition of datasets, for example, through technologies that guarantee data security and privacy.

5.2 Data Management System

Data Management System start-ups address data organization and support the integration and preparation phases. Furthermore, they propose solutions for data governance activities, for data security issues, and for the related compliance with regulations. They make up 18% of the start-ups surveyed and are divided into five subcategories:

Database Management System: Technologies and languages through which to collect and store big data.

Data Integration Systems: Start-ups that facilitate the integration of data from different sources and/or heterogeneous formats.

Data Quality and Preparation Systems: Solutions dedicated to guaranteeing data quality and simplifying data preparation processes.

Data Pipeline Management System: Platforms that support the creation of complex data pipelines, i.e., cleaning raw data for subsequent analysis, to view insights.

Security and Privacy System: Start-ups that simplify and guarantee security, integrity, and respect for privacy in data processing.

5.2.1 General Analytics System

General analytics system start-ups offer solutions aimed at analyzing general-purpose data from the point of view of the objective of the analysis, supporting the phases of the data life cycle and allowing the user to pursue different objectives based on different data sources. They make up 48% of the sample and are divided into three subcategories:

Analytics Platform: Platforms that, through the integration of different technologies, support the management of the end-to-end analytics process, i.e., the data life cycle, from the ingestion of data from numerous systems to data preparation to analysis of the different types of data sources. Furthermore, they allow the creation of dashboards and reports.

Data Science and AI Platform: Solutions for the development of Advanced Analytics, for the enabling of programs in different languages and for the development of Machine Learning and Deep Learning algorithms, thanks to the integration with open-source frameworks and libraries. Such start-ups also offer several features to accelerate collaboration within the Data Science team.

Data Exploration System: Systems for the graphic representation of data in complex and multidimensional visual formats.

5.2.2 Vertical Analytics System

Finally, the remaining 23% of the sample is made up of Vertical Analytics System start-ups, i.e., innovative start-ups that deal with the management of specific end-to-end Analytics data and processes, such as Social Analytics or IoT Analytics.

If it is true that the first to grasp its potential were big players, such as Amazon, Apple, Facebook, and Google, who decided to base their business on the ability to use the enormous amount of data available to them, to date, the intuition has also been followed by numerous start-up companies to grow the global big data market, as previously mentioned. Moreover, there are studies that show that the data recovered from large companies can also help identify "innovative SMEs" (Bottai et al., 2022) and start-up companies from a fully open innovation perspective (Chesbrough, 2003).

References

Agrawal, A., Gans, J., & Goldfarb, A. (2017). *What to expect from artificial intelligence*. MIT Sloan Management Review.

Aernoudt, R. (2004). Incubators: Tool for entrepreneurship? *Small Business Economics, 23*(2), 127–135.

Bottai, C., Crosato, L., Domenech, J., Guerzoni, M., & Liberati, C., (2022). *Unconventional data for policy: Using big data for detecting Italian innovative SMEs, proceedings of the 2022 ACM Conference on Information Technology for Social Good.*

Boulton, C. (2018). *What is digital transformation? A necessary disruption.* CIO. Retrieved on December 20, 2018.

Bower, J., & Clayton, M. (1995). *Disruptive technologies, Catching the wave.* HBR.

Bounfour, A. (2016). Digital futures, digital transformation. In *Progress in IS* (Vol. 10, pp. 978–973). Springer International Publishing.

Bruneel, J., Ratinho, T., Clarysse, B., & Groen, A. (2012). The evolution of business incubators: Comparing demand and supply of business incubation services across different incubator generations. *Technovation, 32*(2), 110–121.

Behl, A., Dutta, P., Lessmann, S., et al. (2019). A conceptual framework for the adoption of big data analytics by e-commerce start-ups: A case-based approach. *Information Systems and e-Business Management, 17*, 285–318.

Chesbrough, H. W. (2003). *Open innovation: The new imperative for creating and profiting from technology.* Harvard Business School Press.

Ciani, N. (2022). *Start-up e big data analytics: La strada verso l'innovazione, Osservatori digital innovation*, Politecnico di Milano.

Davenport, T. H., & Dyché, J. (2013). Big data in big companies. *International Institute for Analytics, 3*(1–31).

Fitzgerald, M., Kruschwitz, N., Bonnet, D., & Welch, M. (2013). *Embracing digital technology: A new strategic imperative.* MIT Sloan Management Review, Research Report.

Kelnar D., (2019) 'The disruptors'—Unique insight into Europe's 1,600 AI start-ups Part2,. MMC Writers.

Kostoff, N., & Boylan, R. (2004). Disruptive technology roadmaps. *Technological Forecasting and Social Change, 71*(1–2), 141.

Maiolini, R., & Giudici, A. (2019). Orchestrare l'innovazione per creare valore sociale. *Sviluppo & Organizzazione, 285*, 40–44.

Marinoni, A., & Voorheis, J. (2019). *Who gains from creative destruction?: Evidence from high-quality entrepreneurship in the United States.* US Census Bureau.

MISE. (2020).

MISE. (2021).

MMC Venture. (2019). Website of British Ventur Capital Firm. www.mmc.vc

Moore, G. (2016). *Crossing the chasm.* Harper Business Essentials United States.

Nielsen, C., & Lund, M. (2018). The concept of business model scalability. *Journal of Business Model., 6*, 1.

Onetti A., (2014), When does a start-up turn into a Scaleup,. Mind the bridge.

Petretto, L. (2007). *Imprenditore ed Università nello start up di impresa, ruoli e relazioni critiche.* Firenze University Press.

Priestley, D. (2018). *Entrepreneur revolution: How to develop your entrepreneurial mindset and start a business that works.* John Wiley & Sons.

Ries, E. (2011). *The lean start-up: How today's entrepreneurs use continuous innovation to create radically successful businesses.* Currency.

Sole24Ore. (2019).

Seggie, S. H., Soyer, E., & Pauwels, K. H. (2017). Combining big data and lean start-up methods for business model evolution. *AMS Review, 7*(3), 154–169.

Stolterman, E., & Fors, A. (2004). Information technology and the good life. *Information Systems Research*, 687–692.

Thiel. (2014). From zero to One, Blake.

Zaki, M., & Hussein, A. (2019). A survey on vertical and horizontal scaling platforms for big data analytics. *International Journal of Integrated Engineering, 11*(6).

Part II
Benchmarking for Start-up Ecosystems

International Benchmark for Italian Start-Up Ecosystems

1 Introduction

The enormous contrasts between the ecosystems of Italy and the Mediterranean and those found outside might also indicate the strategic value of benchmarking with global best practices.

In this chapter, the author of the book investigates the key themes in the wider context of the most relevant start-up ecosystems, in particular three start-up ecosystems, aiming to acquire practical insights into the activities they performed. We chose three start-up ecosystems that were very different from each other. The first two are Italian ecosystems with opposite functioning models but inserted in a similar economic and cultural context. The third, probably the most important in the world, that of San Francisco, Silicon Valley, was chosen because it operates in a practically opposite cultural economic scenario.

The first two chosen start-up ecosystems are not even mentioned in the main global reports on international start-up ecosystems (i.e., Global Report Genome), and the third ranks first in the ranking of the same report.

As support for the development of the three case studies, our choice is in line with previous studies in entrepreneurship, such as Goyal et al. (2016), opting for a qualitative and exploratory approach (Hernández & González, 2016) that concerns different steps and levels of analysis. We start by framing the different contexts taken into consideration through referenced reports and then analyze them in detail by calibrating some interviews with ecosystem actors following the narrative analysis approach (Boje, 1991). Finally, we compare the results to start the benchmarking activity.

F. Greco, *Startup Ecosystems*, Studies on Entrepreneurship, Structural Change and Industrial Dynamics, https://doi.org/10.1007/978-3-031-34414-5_6

2 Drivers for Analysis: Actors, Contexts, and Resources

As a result of combining the data from the Global Start-up Ecosystem Genome and other referenced reports with insights from the literature, it was possible to identify the themes mentioned in Table 1 as having a significant influence on the discussion of start-up ecosystems.

The table lists the key references from start-up ecosystems, such as Genome (2022), and from the literature, as well as the tangible objects that emerged from each subject and shaped the questions.

The author uses the three points of view to characterize the ecosystems already used in previous research (Greco & Tregua, 2022). These are represented by the themes and perspectives investigated and reported in the table: Actor, Context, and Resource. The salient contents are the outputs of the analysis of the genome report, indispensable for guiding the semistructured interviews with the main players of the identified ecosystems.

The following subsections reveal the most evident results from the infusion process between the Evidence from the Global Reports and the literature.

2.1 Actors of Start-up Ecosystems

According to some scholars, start-up ecosystems provide much attention to actors.

Krajcik and Formanek (2015, p. 15) describe the key role of actors in depicting a start-up ecosystem and its potentialities, as they state that (a) actors such as start-ups, policy agencies, incubators, accelerators, and risk capital providers are structural components, and (b) openness may favor the joining of new actors, as it "is rare to have a complete start-up ecosystem." Similarly, Franco-Leal et al. (2019) describe different stages of a start-up ecosystem, each of which has its own duties and resources; hence, connections with actors are required to cover the gaps relating to both activities to be carried out and resources to be incorporated. Laužikas and Dailydaitė (2015) present a somewhat different perspective, but one that is still based on actors; in fact, they believe that a start-up ecosystem is influenced both by actions taken by its members and by actions taken by outside parties, such as factors that favor the growth of new businesses. Similar to how Sipola et al. (2016) conceptualized this ecosystem, it included players and contextual elements, a temporal dimension, renewal processes, and the preceding economic history and regulations. As is the case in the contribution by Cukier and Kon (2018), to identify regulations, market, finance, knowledge, entrepreneurial capabilities, and entrepreneurial culture as factors affecting the performance of an entrepreneurial ecosystem, the latter topic is not frequently considered in the more established literature.

The institutional dynamic in incubators and accelerators hence favors either the maturing or emergence of businesses (Joshi & Satyanarayana, 2014).

Table 1 Contents, perspectives, and elements to guide the interviews. (Reworking by the author)

Variables identified	Key elements	Major citations from Genome	Major citations in the literature
Overview of the ecosystem	Nature, data on start-ups, ongoing activities	Ranking of the best ecosystems with description of selection metrics	Kanbach & Stubner (2016) Cukier & Kon (2018)
Actors shaping the start-up ecosystems	Universities, senior UBA administrators, active start-ups, scaled-up versions of past start-ups, and fundraisers	Collaboration with universities (San Diego); Scale-up globally (Mid-East Region)	Breznitz & Zhang (2019) Krajcik & Formanek (2015) Hernández & González (2016) Mansoori et al. (2019)
Context hosting the activities of the ecosystem	Support from the community, regional economic, social and cultural backdrop, setting, and information environment	Local innovation market (Madrid); Supportive community (Boston)	Bernhofer & Han (2014) Cukier et al. (2016) Sipola et al. (2016)
Resources offered to start-ups a) In general	Core competence, technical resources, prestige, Venture Capital interplay among resources, structures	Artificial intelligence Labs (Montréal); Talent attraction (Seoul)	Buchnik et al. (2018) Franco-Leal et al. (2019) Malecki (2018) Stayton & Mangematin (2019)
b) Knowledge-based activities	Learning-focused, innovative, and supportive of strategy (including exit)	Knowledge through connections (Rhineland); From higher education to bootstrap (Western Denmark)	Dempwolf et al. (2014) Tripathi et al. (2019)
c) Relationship	Market connections, collaboration support	Interplay between local-global markets (Nur-Sultan); Partnership and co-opetition with big players (Belgrade and NoviSad)	Berger & Kuckertz (2016) Bliemel & Flores (2015) Baloutsos et al. (2020)

We may thus conclude from the literature and a review of the reports that the actors shaping the start-up ecosystem and the UBA include universities, UBA directors and other key individuals, start-ups now engaged, past companies that have scaled up, and fundraisers. Collaboration with universities (San Diego) and scaling up internationally are two instances and the key references from Genome (Mid-East Region).

2.2 Context of Start-up Ecosystems

However, other scholars contend that start-up ecosystems adapted a viewpoint depending on geographical factors. Cukier et al. (2016) defined a start-up ecosystem as "a limited region within 30 miles (or one-hour travel range), formed by people, their start-ups, and various types of supporting organizations, interacting as a complex system to create new start-up companies." This definition is one of the contributions of adopting this strategy. This is similar to Cohen (2006), who identified the "diverse collection of interdependent actors within a geographic region that impact the development and final trajectory of the entire group of actors [. . .] to produce new venture creation over time" in the proposal of his view on a start-up ecosystem (pp. 2–3). A few years later, Bernhofer and Han (2014) concentrated on the social and cultural context as factors that support innovation and personal characteristics; as a result, due to the inner nature of start-ups, with innovation and the personality of the entrepreneur at their core, the authors describe the start-up ecosystems evolving over time because of the outcomes of innovation and the personal features of the entrepreneurs, the majority of them depending on the local context. In any case, this environment may seem chaotic, which presents a "difficult in the challenge" for would-be businesses.

The socioeconomic, institutional, and informational environments of a city influence the start-up ecosystem and the companies themselves, according to a more focused perspective (Audretsch & Belitski, 2017). As a result, cities are settings for hosting start-ups. Similarly, by examining rural situations, Miles and Morrison (2020) reinforced this notion; they see these settings as being present in both the steps that lead to the development of a company and the operations it carries out.

According to the findings and the literature, we can thus conclude that the geographic context hosting the ecosystem's activities is the accelerator's business model and profitability. The local innovation market in Madrid and the supportive community in Boston are two major examples of Genome.

2.3 Resources of Start-up Ecosystems

The third category of contributions offers a view of the resources that are forming and influencing the start-up ecosystem and explains it.

Spiegel made a groundbreaking contribution concentrating on resources by describing the entrepreneurial culture, financial rewards, and other characteristics of an industrial culture as catalysts for new initiatives. Knowledge and risk capital are given much weight in this field as resources assisting in the creation of an environment for start-ups and influencing the success of transformation (Hemmert et al., 2019).

Malecki (2018) further said that an ecosystem's nature is that of an umbrella in terms of both word and context; as a result, an ecosystem is a setting made up of resources and supporting activities as a result of them. Similarly, Buchnik et al. (2018) claim that the effectiveness of a start-up ecosystem depends on the many resources accessible, both those linked to new firms and those that are common to all enterprises (such resources, knowledge, and skills) (such as contests, simulations, a learning program via lectures, and mentoring). The permeability of new expertise, extra players, and new ways of doing things is favored by the fluidity of start-up ecosystems, which in turn gives them a boost. Finally, innovative methods for resource integration and reciprocal exchange serve as stimuli for entrepreneurs. All these components are necessary for an environment focused on innovation (Fraiberg, 2017; Ventura et al., 2020), but more research is needed to show how start-up communities may be enhanced and how accelerator members can influence companies and start-up ecosystems (Cohen et al., 2019).

Considering the literature and studies, we can thus say that the resources provided by actors to start-ups are as follows:

- In General: Some key references from the Genome study are Artificial intelligence Labs (Montréal), Talent recruitment (Seoul), and core competencies, technological resources, prestige, interplay among resources, and structures.
- Knowledge-based activities: A focus on innovation and learning; some key references from Genome Knowledge via connections (Rhineland); a strategic support framework that includes departure; from a university education to self-sufficiency (Western Denmark).
- Relationship: market connections, assistance for collaborations. Several key references from Genome include Partnerships with major companies and Interplay between local and global markets (Nur-Sultan) (Belgrade and NoviSad).

3 Rome's Start-Up Ecosystem

As also stated in the paragraph dedicated to the benchmark with the San Francisco ecosystem of excellence, it is not very reliable to refer solely to the analysis of the register of innovative start-ups to understand their distribution and proliferation throughout the country. It would be more appropriate to observe where specialized actors are concentrated, such as incubators, accelerators, universities involved, and start-up operating territories. This analysis shows that there are many intermediates in Rome operators with a tendency to grow, and among these are only international operators operating in Italy. Rome is therefore the city with the greatest concentration of public or private incubators and accelerators in Italy, followed by Milan. The Roma Start-up Association declares that every year, more than 100 innovative start-ups in Rome participate in incubation or acceleration projects: most of these receive funding ranging from 300 thousand to one million euros. In addition to initiatives specifically dedicated to the sector, the city of Rome, with its 28 universities, is the largest Italian campus.

To provide insights, the author consulted various reports, including those of the association "Roma Start-up Association," "Lazio Innova," Cerved-Italia Start-up, and Deelroom.

The consultation of the aforementioned reports demonstrates evidence regarding the increase in interest on the part of the institutions in the start-up ecosystem of the city.

The liveliness of the scene is also demonstrated by the very high number of specialized events aimed at the community of innovators taking place in Rome and by their success in terms of visitors and speakers.

The activation of these activities of local observers allows the Roman ecosystem to benefit. Not only does it allow for the mapping and snapshot of the state of the art, but it also allows for the identification of new development paths.

3.1 Metrics

This analysis demonstrates how swiftly Rome's start-up environment has expanded in recent years. There are increasingly more corporate, governmental, and international initiatives to encourage creative entrepreneurship in the region. From the first Private Accelerator opened in 2010, in 2021, the city showed 25 incubators/accelerators, 12 FabLabs, 5 Technology Transfer Centres, and 50 Smart Working Centres. In addition, over 20 associations and institutions with specific programs to accompany young innovative companies contribute to spreading the technology culture in Rome (Rome Start-up Association, 2021).

Furthermore, in 2019, 14 start-ups worked together in Rome (Economy up, 2019). To date, Rome registers 1138 start-ups.

Every year, in the city, there are a hundred start-ups participating in incubation or acceleration programs, and most of them receive funding from 300 K to 1 M in euros.

Between the end of 2019 and the beginning of 20,020, there were 4000 start-ups in Rome (Start-up Business, 2020).

3.2 Supporting Players: Accelerator and Incubator in Rome

Below, we propose a mapping of the main incubators and accelerators in Rome:

1. Luiss Enlabs.

   Start-up accelerator in Rome managed by Lventure Group, a venture capital company that provides Luiss Enlabs start-ups with financing and networks.

   Luiss En Labs is one of the leading start-up accelerators in Europe. Born in 2013 from a joint venture between LVenture Group, a listed venture capital operator, and LUISS University, in just a few years, it has supported the growth of over 40 start-ups. Its headquarters, a coworking space of approximately 5000 square meters, is in a strategic location in the historic wing of Rome's Termini Station.
2. "Spazio Attivo di Lazio Innova Roma Tecnopolo".

   The "Spazio Attivo Roma Tecnopolo" is an incubator for the creation and development of new companies with high technological content. Since 2006, it has been the seat of the ESA BIC Lazio Incubator, born from the agreement between the Lazio Region, the European Space Agency (ESA) and the Italian Space Agency (ASI), within the Technology Transfer Program (TTP) of the European Space Agency. The goal is to facilitate the use of space technologies and systems for innovative commercial applications (products and/or services). The program includes incubation and financial support for start-ups.
3. Picampus.

   Picampus is an incubator for early-stage start-ups; it is a space surrounded by greenery in the heart of the Eur district of Rome, which combines the best working environment with talented realities.

   Pi Campus is both a start-up district and a venture fund that invests in talent.

   This incubator provides start-ups with money, mentoring and the best possible working environment to grow them. The organization began in the base of a single luxury residential villa where two companies were based: Translated, the first Internet-based translation service, and Memopal, a backup technology provider used by manufacturers of storage, telecommunications, and antivirus services.
4. Start-upbootcamp Foodtech.

   Start-upbootcamp Foodtech is the first global Food Tech accelerator based in Rome. Launches a call to select start-ups active in the field of technologies applied to the world of food to be hosted and accelerated in the complex a few tens of meters from the Basilica of San Giovanni.
5. Italia Camp.

   Italia Camp promotes and supports business creations in the field of social innovation and the development of new answers to real questions, working to bridge the gap between the birth of an idea and its realization.

   We could define it as one of the first "social incubators" in Italy to believe in the idea of putting the person and their social relationships at the center to generate new value in terms of economic and social impact for communities and territories.

3.3 The Commitment of the University and Public Support

Rome is the largest campus in Europe for a number of university students: 28 universities for a total of 300,000 students. Among the most renowned universities, Rome has • John Cabot University • LUISS • Università La Sapienza • LUMSA • Università Campus Bio-Medico Roma • Università degli Studi di Roma "Tor Vergata" • Università Roma Tre • Libera Università degli Studi per l'Innovazione e le Organizzazioni.

Thanks to the large number of universities present in the city, Rome is the city in Italy with more courses dealing with entrepreneurship.

This, along with the fact that most of these courses are held in English, is one of the reasons why Rome is the second most sought-after destination in the world by students from the United States (immediately after London).

We see, below, some main university initiatives to support the development of start-ups:

1. Dok3.

   At Roma Tre University, the engineering department, in collaboration with the Dock-3 incubator The Start-up Lab offer during the Rome Start-up Week, a program that lasts 5 months with a first bimonthly training phase, followed by the course of actual incubation. Everyone can participate, students and workers, just be motivated, be linked in some way to the university and know-how to work in a team. Dock-3 is also aimed at those who do not yet have their own business idea. This can be born in Dock3Jam, in comparison with mentors and aspirants
2. Rome Start-up Weekend at John Cabot University.

   The penultimate event of the start-up week before COVID-19 was held in 2019 at John Cabot University in Rome.

   Under the patronage of Associazione Nazionale Giovani Innovatori and the Canadian Chamber in Italy, John Cabot University invited students, associate professors, and professors to participate in the JCU Weekend of Start-ups in 2019 and for the third consecutive year.

   The event is aimed at promoting entrepreneurship and entrepreneurial culture by involving university students and young entrepreneurs, start-uppers, designers, and developers. It is the latter who engage in a competition of entrepreneurial creativity and innovation, presenting innovative ideas and creating a work team to develop the project, all within 54 h and thanks to the support of experienced mentors and coaches. The ideas generated during the "marathon" will then be presented to a jury who will decide the winners of the contest, awarding prizes aimed at promoting the start-up of the business.
3. "Porta futura Lazio".

   Porta Futura Lazio is the project of the Lazio Region, public and free, created in collaboration with the universities that offer everyone the opportunity to grow professionally, through guidance and training services, to position themselves better on the job market. In recent years, Porta Futura Lazio has dedicated a great deal of effort to the start-up ecosystem with various initiatives, including collaboration with Forma Camera, in organizing the Business Start-Up seminar. This workshop provides information on how to evaluate a business idea and how to find the financial means to launch it. A workshop designed to help avoid making the most common mistakes when starting a start-up.

Regarding the support of the public administration of Rome, it should be reported that "*Local both the Lazio Region and the Municipality of Rome are sustaining the flourishment of the start-up ecosystem in the territory. The Lazio Region has introduced the following tools:*

- *cancellation of local additional corporate tax on start-ups.*
- *grant program, doubling private investor's preseeds (30 k–100 k euro at the idea stage).*
- *VC fund matching 2.5x on private investments (up to 2.5 million euro each);*
- *"a small fund of funds". The City of Rome is mapping its available spaces to be turned in smart working spaces and it is working with private operators to create a public–private investment agency."*[1]

3.4 The Main Start-Ups in Rome

Start-up name: Big Profiles.

Industry: Finance, Big Data, AI.

Headquarters: Rome.

What they do: Big profiles (Roma tre University) starts from the basic information on customers available to companies and then enriches it with other data packages acquired from social networks, open data and other data sources to map people in a detailed way. In such a way that banks and insurance companies can redefine the customer target and develop the best marketing strategies.

Start-up name: On Charge.

Industry: E-mobility, Green Economy.

Headquarters: Rome.

What they do: ON Charge is the first start-up in Italy to enter the world of electric vehicle charging and sharing mobility. The goal of this start-up is to strengthen the segment of sustainable and electric mobility, private and shared, starting from Rome, creating truly sustainable and electric mobility hubs, responding to market demands and travel needs ecological and safe from a health point of view.

Start-up name: Genome Up.

Industry: Health, AI.

Headquarters: Rome.

What they do: Genome Up is an innovative start-up that has developed artificial intelligence (AI) to support hospitals, laboratories, and research centers to find, in

[1] These contents have been collected from the pages of the Lazio Region website (Lazioinnova.it).

less than 24 h, the most accurate diagnosis and therapy for patients with rare diseases through the analysis of DNA.

Start-up name: MyBiros.

Industry: E Learning.

Headquarters: Rome.

What they do: MyBiros, a tool that uses deep learning techniques to extract information from any document: printed and manuscript. Unlike traditional solutions, MyBiros recognizes the text, understands, and extracts the fields of interest.

Start-up name: OffLunch.

Industry: Food Delivery, Marketplace, AI.

Headquarters: Rome.

What they do: OFFLunch is the first food delivery service designed specifically for the lunch break in the office to have a healthy, balanced, economical menu every day with punctual and free delivery.

4 The Start-Up Ecosystem of Naples: Numbers and an Overview

When, in Italy, we talk about start-ups, innovation, and new business creation, we immediately think of Milan and northern Italy. In fact, the birth of new businesses in the South is still slow, and certified incubators in the South are few: out of 45 incubators in Italy, only 5 are in the Center or South (Infocamere, 2021). In the face of all this, however, the Campania region shows decidedly countertrend and growing data. The growing trend is evident, and it is demonstrated by the important initiatives at local level, just think of the "Unione degli Industriali" which created the Digital innovation hub or the University Federico II, an established reality both from the point of view of the transfer of typical skills and of innovation: the Apple Academy is considered a best practice from all over Italy. The Cisco Digital Transformation Lab in Naples should also be mentioned, born from the collaboration between Cisco and Federico II University. The attractiveness of the Naples start-up ecosystem is also demonstrated by the establishment of some large players.

For example, Ferrovie dello Stato recently built a hub in San Giovanni a Teduccio. This is the first after that of Rome. Then, there is the academy dedicated to 5G, where a few well-known big players are concentrated, from Nokia to Tim. Finally, the Apple Academy, as already reported, is now a consolidated success reality.

Although in the North there are dizzying numbers in relation to the birth of new businesses and the South is still lagging, there is a noteworthy countertrend: Campania is the third region of Italy for the number of start-ups, (Registrodelleimprese.it), and the first among the southern regions. Naples also achieves an excellent position. The latest MISE report at the end of 2021 showed Naples as the third Italian city for registered start-up companies; specifically, there are 607, 4.47% of the total Italian start-ups. They deal with space applications and software, or 3D printing, 4.0 technologies, and algorithms to support digital, biomedical, and pharmaceutical marketing. They arise from a system that has developed into a network built around seven universities, 40 advanced research public bodies, 21 laboratories, and 25 structures to support entrepreneurship, including accelerators, science parks, and service centers (Sole 24 ore, 2019). What is still missing is above all the investment in the capital of the youngest and most immature start-ups. The study by Zephiro and Campania Newsteel 18 certified incubator of the city of Naples also gives clear indications on this issue. Between 2018 and 2019, investment in "seed capital" decreased in Campania to less than 5% of the total, and the city of Naples also witnessed this negative trend.

4.1 The University Federico II in the Start-Up Ecosystem of Naples

The presence and role of the first University of the city of Naples (University of Naples Federico II) is remarkable. The intervention of the Universities of Campania is active in most activities and institutional bodies. In addition to being a partner of the first certified incubator in Southern Italy, present in Naples, Campania New Steel, Federico II University is engaged in many local initiatives to provide support for the birth and development of start-ups and the proliferation of the ecosystem. The University of Naples Federico II participates in networks and awards aimed at supporting those who develop business ideas based on research and innovation.

The mapping that we will show highlights the university's commitment to both internal university initiatives and collaborations with external organizations, both public and private. The series of initiatives and organizations reported shows the increase in awareness on the part of the university on the importance of investing in training and support for the creation of new businesses.

4.1.1 Campania NewSteel

Campania NewSteel, is the first incubator in the South, promoted and participated by the University of Naples Federico II and certified by the Mise pursuant to the Growth Decree 2.0.

To date, at the incubator, there are 20 Innovative Start-ups 33 Accelerated Projects 150 Employed 11 million Ecosystem turnover 750 K Innovative start-up funding.

Campania New Steel (CNS) was founded in November 2016 with the members of the University of Naples Federico II and Città della Scienza, which has conferred the spaces and curriculum of its business incubator operating since 2003. In June 2017, it obtained certification pursuant to growth decree 2.0, the only one in southern Italy out of the 38 certificates in Italy.

In its offer system, the incubator provides support services and specialized services to allow start-ups that are set up to better integrate into the ecosystem, facilitating access to the market and funds, multiplying relationships and opportunities, promoting international development supporting the creation and development of start-up, spinoff, and restart-up projects engaged in its strategic reference clusters.

4.1.2 Start Cup Campania

Start Cup Campania is the Innovation Award promoted by Campania universities and aimed at competing groups of people who develop business ideas based on research and innovation.

It is a real business plan competition whose objective is to support research and technological innovation aimed at economic development and the creation of companies with high knowledge content. The competition is part of the National Innovation Award (PNI), a similar competition organized nationally by various Italian universities, in which the winners of local editions take part. For the 2020 edition, there was operational coordination at the University Service Center for the Coordination of Special Projects and Organizational Innovation (COINOR) of the University of Naples Federico II. For the nomination of the starr cup award, a scientific committee is appointed that evaluates the business projects presented with reference to the following general criteria:

(a) Originality of the business idea.
(b) Value of the technological or knowledge content.
(c) Feasibility.
(d) Development potential and project ambition.
(e) Adequacy of skills of the management team.
(f) Attractiveness of the reference market.
(g) Quality and completeness of documentation.

4.1.3 Federico II University Spin-off Commission

The Federico II University of Naples (hereinafter referred to as the "University") promotes the achievement of its institutional goals and promotes and supports technology transfer and research enhancement activities.

In this scenario, it often happens that groups of researchers, often from universities (a particularly widespread phenomenon in the United States), decide to undertake a path of commercial development of the results of their work, launching corporate initiatives known as spin-offs. In this way, precious energies are invested in processes aimed at further developing knowledge and seeking markets interested in using it and paying for it, generating a virtuous circuit of resources and individual and collective benefits. Spin-offs can be of two types: "participated spin offs" in which the university participates as a member and "nonparticipated spin offs" in which the university does not have a share.

In recent years, the commission has preferred to proceed in all cases with modalities such as "nonparticipated spin offs."

University can be attributed to a company already established if all the conditions provided for by this regulation and by current legislation are met. The qualification of spin-off can be attributed upon proposal of the company concerned within 4 years of its establishment. The participation of university staff in the spin-off can take place both in terms of participation in the capital and in terms of direct commitment to achieving the corporate purpose, offering the new legal entity the use of the know-how and skills generated in a context of research.

4.1.4 Italian Scouts in Silicon Valley

From 2014 to 2017, promoted by DEMI Federico II in collaboration with the Ministry of Foreign Affairs, the Italian Consulate of San Francisco, and the Union of Industrialists of Naples.

The "Italian Scouts in Silicon Valley" project was created to better recognize and understand the opportunities that can arise from the interaction between the Italian fabric of innovative entrepreneurship and the Silicon Valley innovation ecosystem.

Through cultural, scientific research, and business scouting activities, the project has made it possible to highlight the strengths, the opportunities connected to Silicon Valley, and the actors best suited to exploit them.

Through the information of the Consulate General of Italy in San Francisco, it was possible to analyze the structure of the Italian start-up in Silicon Valley, working on a sample of 65 companies out of the hundred existing:

Almost 50% of start-ups have been established in the last 2 years (2014–2015). Forty percent have fewer than 10 employees, and 90% have fewer than 50. They are mainly active in the ICT sector. Only 15% of the start-ups considered are university spin-offs. The companies surveyed raised $ 645 million in funding. For 60% of start-ups, funding ranges from 0 to 2 million dollars. The founders are aged between 30 and 40 (50% of the total) or over 40 (40%). They have an Italian master's degree and 18% a research doctorate. In 40% of cases, they are on their second experience as a founder.

4.1.5 Start N'up

Start N'Up, the program promoted by Unione Industriali and Federico II University, which supports young aspiring entrepreneurs, university spin-offs and companies with high growth potential, becomes operational.

From the Start N'Up platform, it is possible to convey business ideas and/or projects and to obtain information on the start-up phenomenon, on the evolution of the legislation on the subject, on opportunities, tenders, and concessions at the regional, national, and European levels.

The best business ideas and university spin-offs selected by a Technical-Scientific Committee—made up of representatives from the business, university, and finance worlds—can be supported with mentoring interventions by large companies or SMEs associated with the *Unione Industriali* and/or receive assistance/tutoring, free of charge, in financial, tax, notary matters, business plan drafting by a team of authoritative experts. It will be possible, moreover, to compete for the selection foreseen by the Program of *Piccola Industria Confindustria* for the adoption of start-ups.

4.2 Event and Community

4.2.1 Smau

The Smau event is a reference for companies interested in getting in touch with new partners on open innovation issues. "Start-up Safaris" are organized through Smau, i.e., tours created for organizations with the aim of seeking compatibility between market trends and the offer of the start-ups present. With the start-up Safaris, innovation managers, decision makers, and entrepreneurs can meet start-ups active in various sectors: from agri-food to aerospace, from tech to fashion, from medicine to education up to electronic identity and intelligent mobility.

4.2.2 NA Start Up

NA Start Up is a community that organizes itinerant events in the city of Naples to give the new founders of start-ups the opportunity to meet other companies and possibly network with them. In this way, entrepreneurs, journalists, professionals, geeks, curious, technicians, programmers, industrialists, etc., meet to follow the speeches of the start-up representatives.

At the end of the presentations, a Wi-Fi-based system allows participants to vote and win the proposal they liked the most. Victory is not rewarded with money or contracts but, in line with the spirit of the initiative, with greater visibility. Visibility, however, is guaranteed to all participants.

4.2.3 TIM W Cap

In the San Giovanni a Teduccio University Complex, Federico II hosts the Innovation Hub born from the collaboration between TIM and Cisco Italy, world leader in the networking and IT sectors. This translates into a demo area dedicated to Industry 4.0, Smart City, Cyber Security, and Multi Cloud, and equipped with platforms and technological assets available to design, develop, and test new applications in these sectors.

The choice of location is designed to foster osmosis between the academic and industrial worlds.

4.2.4 Napoli Start-Up Weekend

Naples was home to one of the largest international start-up events: Start-up Weekend, which is a 3-day program where aspiring entrepreneurs can experience start-up life. The participating startups come from all over the world.

The event, conceived by the American Andrew Hyde, includes a 54-h marathon in which all participants develop their business idea in a single weekend with the help of mentors and industry professionals.

The last edition in 2017 was won by Sheralo, a web platform for sharing disused objects with a high potential for creative recycling.

4.3 Main Start-Ups in Naples Start-Up Ecosystem

Start-up name: *Megaride.*

Industry: Automotive, A.I.

Headquarters: Naples.

What they do: A software house that develops algorithms to simulate what happens when a racing car or a motorcycle is launched on the track at maximum speed. Megaride was founded in 2016 as a software house, testing center, and smart mobility provider, with the aim of becoming a reference point in the development of advanced models for real-time simulation of vehicle dynamics on the road, in the automotive and motorsport sectors, and in the supply of software products for the optimization of vehicle performance and smart mobility.

Start-up name: *Unobravo.*

Industry: Mental Health.

Headquarters: Naples.

What they do: They operate in the mental health sector and offer an online psychology service in Italian: the team is made up of several psychologists who work exclusively via video call. The service is specially designed for Italians abroad, who find it difficult to find psychological support, in Italian, in the country where they are: therefore, the interviews are done remotely. Then, an innovative matching algorithm comes into play, which favors meeting with the most suitable therapist and personal affinities and needs identified with the previous questionnaire.

Start-up name: *Buzzoole.*

Industry: Social influencer Marketing, A.I.

Headquarters: Naples.

What they do: Buzzoole is an influencer marketing solution provider that is able to connect brands to content creators using artificial intelligence. Now becoming a scale-up, Buzzoole uses proprietary technology based on artificial intelligence to create the perfect match between Brand and Influencer.

The substantial fundraising obtained has helped to boost the development of a large suite of solutions dedicated to the enterprise market and will integrate the "Discovery tool," a tool that allows companies to autonomously discover and select the content creators to be involved in campaign, enriching it with a further add-on that facilitates brands in tracking their own campaigns and those of their competitors.

Start-up name: *Cogisen.*

Industry: Cognitive A.I.

Headquarters: Naples.

What they do: Cogisen is a Neapolitan start-up born in Naples in 2009. To extract meaning, purpose, and context from video and other inputs, Cogisen created an AI cognitive modelling platform. The company then built mobile and social apps, autonomous cars, and the Internet of Things. With a strong proprietary IP and technology, Cogisen competes in a market for data compression applications that is quickly expanding. Atlante Venture and TT Venture funds both made investments in the business (directly and indirectly through TTSeed Srl). In June 2021, a large Silicon Valley technology corporation purchased Cogisen.

5 The Silicon Valley a Benchmark for Excellence

In this final part of the book, salient aspects of the Silicon Valley ecosystem are described through scientific sources (Bania et al., 1993; Kenney, 2000; Lojek, 2007; Steiber et al., 2016), reports (Chioda & Tripepi, 2019), and personal sources (both direct and documented interviews from previously mentioned sources).

Silicon Valley is undoubtedly the most famous and productive cluster of innovation and entrepreneurship in the world, with success stories such as Google, Facebook, Apple, HP, eBay, PayPal, LinkedIn, and Tesla and with an ability to attract money and human capital from all parts of the world. The evolution of Silicon Valley from a cultivation area to the first region of innovation and creation of start-ups worldwide is complex and very articulated.

At the beginning of the 1900s, a radio system was successfully marketed by a Stanford student, while in 1912, the invention of the vacuum tube, also at Stanford, launched the age of electronics. A few years later, in 1938, one of the most iconic start-ups in Silicon Valley, Hewlett-Packard, was born from the university, producing electronic devices such as oscilloscopes and measuring instruments. In this period, Professor Fred Terman played a fundamental role, serving as professor/mentor and encouraging his students to commercialize their research.

After the Second World War, thanks to the skills developed in several economic sectors, Silicon Valley attracted large companies such as General Electric, Kodak, and IBM, which established research and development centers there.

In 1980, there was a very important event: The federal government initiated a policy that allowed a new wave of business creation. Private investors could finance the commercialization of government-subsidized research. Berkeley and Stanford created their own technology transfer offices to maximize revenues from this opportunity, licensing their research to both large companies and start-ups created primarily by the researchers themselves.

At the beginning of the 1970s, with the birth of "Intel," the venture capital investment approach began for the first time. This era also saw the formation of a group of investors who are the founders of what are now venture companies. In 1976, Steve Jobs and Steve Wozniak founded Apple in a garage in Cupertino, and in 1984, ùjobs launched the Macintosh 128 k, contained in a single elegant body, together with a monitor and disk drive. In 1984, a group of students from Stanford University founded the Cisco System. Yahoo and eBay were born in 1995, while in 1998, Larry Page and Sergey Brin founded the company Google, a year after when the search engine was already born. In 2002, LinkedIn was founded by a former PayPal employee, and in the same year, Elon Musk founded SpaceX. Facebook was born in 2004 within Harvard walls, and Twitter in 2006. In 2007, Apple commercialized the first smartphone: the iPhone 2. In 2010, two students from Stanford University, Kevin Systrom, and Mike Krieger, founded Instagram. In 2012, Elon Musk's SpaceX launched the first commercial flight from the International Space Station. Another big step to report, in 2018, was the first ticket sold by SpaceX for a trip to the moon (Chioda & Tripepi, 2019). Thus, Silicon Valley was born thanks mainly to a business development strategy carried out by Stanford University with the support of the government and businesses (Etzkowitz, 2013).

5.1 The Three Strengths of Silicon Valley

"Silicon Valley was created by three historical forces: technology, culture and capitals" (Berlin, 2017). These three forces continue to sustain it today.

5.1.1 Technology

Since the 1950s, all great technological revolutions have been born in S. Francisco. In Silicon Valley, innovators are very often first movers. This has greatly rewarded this ecosystem. Just think that today it is still the first zone in the world for robotics, artificial intelligence, and the Internet of Things (Table 2).

In the context of the advent of the technologies that have determined the entrepreneurial boom, an important step to report was the foundation of the Shockley Semiconductor Laboratory in 1955. This was the first entrepreneurial initiative that used "silico" to produce the "transistor," which would be the technology thanks to which computers, cell phones, and flat-screen TVs were born. Furthermore, after a few years, seven former employees of the Shockley Semiconductor Laboratory

Table 2 Dates and technologies in brief (Source: Chioda & Tripepi, 2019)

1940	Electronic tools
1950	Microchip
1970	Biotech, computers, video games
1980	Software
1990	Web
2000	Cloud, Mobile, social network
2010	Artificial intelligence, machine learning

founded their own semiconductor company, which can be considered the first real start-up company in contemporary history (Lojek, 2007). The phenomenon described is a clear example of how in this ecosystem each invention already contains the seed of the next one.

5.1.2 Culture

When dealing with the Silicon Valley concept of entrepreneurial culture, it is inevitable to refer to the university as a key player in the dissemination and development of entrepreneurship. Stanford is among the top universities in the world that, for some time now, has been churning out talent that creates new businesses (Petretto, 2007). Many authors who study and describe the positive impact of the University in the Silicon Valley ecosystem give credit to Frederick Terman, (Leslie & Kargon, 1996; Adams, 2018; Etzkowitz, 2022) professor of electrical engineering at Stanford since 1925. Terman uses the land near Stanford University to create the "Stanford-research Industrial Park," a technology park where academics, inventors, and venture capitalists coexist and collaborate daily. This technology park is the headquarters of many companies, such as HP, Next, and Tesla Motors (Chioda & Tripepi, 2019). The "StartX" incubator plays a fundamental role within the Stanford Research Park, and it is a main case study used by Etzkowitz and Zhou (2017) to describe their "Triple Helix Model": University–Industry–Government. The triple helix focuses on "innovation in innovation" and the dynamic to foster an innovation ecosystem through various hybrid organizations. technology transfer offices, venture capital firms, incubators, accelerators, and science parks.

5.1.3 Capitals

The presence of large sums of money to invest in Silicon Valley start-up projects is undoubtedly a decisive resource.

An initial boost to the large concentration of current capital was given by huge "federal capital" initially granted by the Pentagon, which, during the Cold War, invested heavily in technologies such as radar and other advanced electronic systems (Berlin, 2017).

In 1972, the first massive wave of Ventur Capital occurred. In the last 20 years, the main investment funds were born (e.g., Sequoia Capital, Kleiner Perkins Caufield & Byers), which invested in start-ups that then turned into scale-ups and large companies such as Facebook, YouTube, Google, and PayPal (Chioda & Tripepi, 2019). Thanks to these copious investments, the propensity for the concept of risk capital was born, that is, the capital of third parties who choose to finance an innovative project to be able to participate in future economic results without being too afraid of a single bankruptcy.

5.2 *Main Berkley University Program for "connect student entrepreneur with UC Berkeley's start-up ecosystem"*

The section of the University of Berkeley website dedicated to supporting students approaching the world of entrepreneurship is entitled with a very emblematic name "Learn. Build. Fund."

Below is a roundup of initiatives from the University of Berkley to support the entrepreneurial initiatives of students, assistant professors, and professors, divided into five macroareas: Incubator, Student Groups, Entrepreneurship Association, Competitions, Fellowships & Fraternities:

5.2.1 Incubators

- The House
  The House is a start-up institute built for Berkeley and home to Berkeley's founders.
- CITRIS Foundry
  CITRIS Foundry is the University of California accelerator for founders building deep technology companies. Provides seed funding, access to campus labs, and mentorship during our 12-month program.
- Free Ventures
  A semester-level student-run accelerator program for both undergraduate and graduate students. Participants receive two upper-division CS units, need-based funding, industry-specific mentorship, weekly workshops, and workspace.
- Catalyst@Berkeley
  Student-run health tech incubators that help interdisciplinary teams of students develop technical skills and navigate through the design process to develop a viable prototype and business plan to bring it to market.
- SkyDeck
  Incubator program for UC Berkeley start-ups. Provides workspace, unique programming, speaker series, and mentorship. A collaboration between the

College of Engineering, the Haas School of Business, and the Office of the Vice Chancellor for Research Applications in March and September annually.

- Venture Lab

  Incubator program and resource center for undergraduate and graduate students. Provides workspace, personalized mentoring, and a community of student entrepreneurs.

  Twelve Week Spring Semester incubator that takes hackathon projects (from Cal Hacks) and helps turn them into nonprofits, start-ups, and open-source projects.

5.2.2 Student Groups

- Machine Learning at Berkeley (ML@B)

  Student group for everything machine learning at Cal. Members organize events on campus, work with companies on applying ML to industry, and publish papers for moonshot ideas.
- CET Student Association

  Student group organizing speaker series and events relating to entrepreneurship. Part of the Center for Entrepreneurship and Technology.
- Venture Strategy Solutions

  Student consulting group focusing on high-growth start-ups in the Bay Area.
- Computer Science Undergraduate Association

  Computer science clubs are open to all students interested in computer science. Holds a variety of both technical and social events throughout the year, including hackathons, info sessions, social parties, and gaming nights.
- Berkeley IEEE

  Electrical engineering student group. Holds technical workshops and info sessions throughout the year.
- Berkeley Innovation

  Undergraduate human-centered design group. Members come from a wide range of disciplines but share a love of design thinking and innovation. Provides hands-on experience with the entire design process, from conducting user research to building and marketing prototypes. Holds designathons.
- Innovative Design

  Student club for graphic designers and photographers. Conducts a DeCal and holds workshops covering a broad range of design topics.
- Mobile Developers @ Berkeley (MDB)

  Student app development group that works on all mobile development projects (iOS/Android) and has worked on dozens of past tech consulting projects.
- Blueprint

Team of UC Berkeley students that develops pro bono software for nonprofits and promotes technology for social good.

- CodeBase

  Software development clubs build a community of passionate and driven engineers who work together on various industry projects (consulting, development, etc.).

5.2.3 Entrepreneurship Associations

- Berkeley Entrepreneurs Association

  Entrepreneurship associations provide a variety of resources to members. Writes a weekly newsletter featuring job postings. Hosts both formal and informal events.
- Berkeley Postdoctoral Entrepreneurs Program

  Entrepreneurship association for the postdoctoral and graduate communities. Provides tools, mentoring, and a platform for science-business communication to encourage research innovations to move into the marketplace.
- CalFounders

  Entrepreneurship association for UC Berkeley alumni. Holds member-only meetings that serve as an informal advisory board for each entrepreneur's independent companies.

5.2.4 Competitions

- LAUNCH: The UC Berkeley Start-up Competition and Accelerator

  Accelerator and competition for early-stage UC-affiliated start-ups. Provides a rigorous curriculum from world-class faculty, intensive mentoring, and the tools to get to fundable.
- Cal Hacks

  Yearly collegiate hackathon for students interested in creating new software and hardware products. Lasts 36 h and takes place in the fall semester.
- Big Ideas@Berkeley

  Annual social impact start-up competition. Provides funding, support, and encouragement to interdisciplinary teams of students. Run by the Blum Center.
- Global Social Venture Competition

  Annual social impact business plan competition. Run collaboratively with a number of universities around the world and the Lester Center.

5.2.5 Fellowships and Fraternities

- Kairos Society Fellowship
  Entrepreneurship fellowships connect like-minded individuals to help members achieve their entrepreneurial goals. Provides one-on-one mentorship and resources to members. Hosts both internal and external events.
- Haas Venture Fellows
  A select group of Berkeley MBA students at the Haas School of Business who do real-world projects to strengthen ties between Bay Area entrepreneurs, the venture capital industry, and the Lester Center.
- Accel Scholars
  Joint program run by Accel and UC Berkeley EECS department that empowers undergraduate engineering students through access to Silicon Valley mentorship and curriculum.[2]

5.3 The Main Start-Ups of the Moment in Silicon

Start-up name: Wing.

Industry: Drone.

Headquarters: Palo Alto, Silicon Valley.

What they do: Being a part of Alphabet, the organization that owns Google, gives Wing a fantastic chance to flourish. They have been able to manufacture and deploy their drone planes for product delivery on three continents because of the substantial money they have already access to.

This start-up has been selected among "the 18 Top Silicon Valley Start-ups to Watch in 2023" according to Statupsavan.[3]

Start-up name: Dremio.

Industry: Big Data.

Headquarters: Santa Clara, Silicon Valley.

What they do: Dremio offers a lakehouse platform that makes it simple to access open data. One advantage of Dremio is that businesses may utilize open-source processing engine standards such as Apache Iceberg and Apache Arrow. Focusing on the context of business intelligence, Dremio allows both data analysts and data scientists to create high-performance BI dashboards.

This start-up has been selected among "the 18 Top Silicon Valley Start-ups to Watch in 2023" according to Statupsavan.[4]

Start-up name: Impossible Foods.

Industry: Plant-Based Foods.

---

[2] This section adopts a major portion of its content from https://startup.berkeley.edu/. CC BY 3.0.

[3] https://start-upsavant.com

[4] Ibidem.

Headquarters: Monte Casino-Patrick Brown, Silicon Valley.

What they do: Impossible Foods, one of the industry's foremost innovators in sustainable food, is on a quest to totally replace animal goods with its succulent plant-based meats. Over 17,000 restaurants and grocery shops nationwide now sell its signature item, the Impossible Burger. With every mouthful, consumers may select meat, dairy, and fish substitutes that benefit the environment.

This start-up has been selected among "the 18 Top Silicon Valley Start-ups to Watch in 2023" according to Statupsavan.[5]

Start-up name: People.ai.

Industry: Artificial Intelligence.

Headquarters: San Francisco, Silicon Valley.

What they do: Artificial intelligence (AI) is being used by People.ai to increase the productivity of sales teams. Their technology assists sales representatives by offering data-driven recommendations on whom to speak, what to say, and when. Companies may shorten sales cycles and improve closing rates using People.ai, which will increase sales and lower marketing expenses.

This start-up has been selected among "the 18 Top Silicon Valley Start-ups to Watch in 2023" according to Statupsavan.[6]

Start-up name: Stripe.

Industry: Digital payments, Fintech.

Headquarters: San Francisco, Silicon Valley.

What they do: In September 2019, before Covid advanced e-commerce by years in a few weeks, Stripe was bypassing WeWork and Airbnb to become America's largest unicorn. A year and a half later, in March 2021, the value of the company founded by brothers Patrick and John Collison (who in 2020 was among the richest under 30 in the world), which provides software infrastructures for Internet payments to individuals and companies, almost tripled. After a $600 million funding round, its valuation rose to $95 billion.

This start-up was selected from a Forbes article declaring it the start-up that became the first unicorn in the United States.[7]

Start-up name: Instacart.

Industry: Grocery delivery.

Headquarters: San Francisco, Silicon Valley.

What they do: Instacart is a kind of Grocery Uber. Potential grocery buyers sign up and download the Instacart app so they can deliver groceries to their local customers. Sometimes customers can also request their favorite Instacart grocery shopper. After the $ 265 million funding round ended in March, the value of the

[5] Ibidem.

[6] Ibidem.

[7] forbes.it

grocery delivery app jumped to $ 39 billion. Its founder is Apoorva Mehta, whose assets are estimated by Forbes at $ 3.5 billion.

This start-up has been called an American unicorn by Forbes.[8]

6 Evidence from Interviews

The author reports a selection of interviews made by him and content that can be traced back to some interviews available in the public domain.

The contents of the interviews were as follows:

University professors who address the ecosystems of interest in this book.

(a) Directors of Incubators and Accelerators of ecosystems of interest to this book.
(b) University professors who deal with entrepreneurship of the ecosystems of interest in this book.
(c) Founders of Start-ups or Scale-ups dealing with entrepreneurship of the ecosystems of interest of this book.
(d) Other influential personalities such as investors and serial managers of the ecosystems of interest to this book.

6.1 Main Evidence from the Interviews with the Directors of Certified Italian Incubators (Rome and Naples)

In this paragraph, we will report the main information obtained from the interviews with the two managers of start-up incubators in Rome (Luiss en Labs—LEL) and in Naples (Campania New Steel—CNS) with respect to the 3 dimensions identified in the previous table of start-up ecosystems: Actor, Resource, and Geographic Context:

Both research contexts are UBAs, but as anticipated, and as will be further described below, they have opposite models. Furthermore, data on already-accelerated start-ups are useful for describing a specialization of the two accelerators. The main businesses of these start-ups by CNS address digital transformation, the implementation of artificial intelligence, the use of the opportunities offered by the Internet of Things, or leveraging the combination of social innovation and health. On the other hand, the main businesses of the start-ups accelerated by LEL are digital transformation, marketplace, and software development.

Another interesting element is a past-looking one—namely, the achievements of start-ups accelerated in CNS and LEL. The number of start-ups of the CNS accelerator that achieved significant fundraising is approximately 15. The total capital raised by start-ups in the CNS accelerator is over 2 million euros. The start-up that

[8] Ibidem.

raised the most funds is SyenMaint, with total fundraising of 250,000€. On the other hand, 80% of start-ups accelerated by LEL managed to raise at least 300,000€. The start-up that has collected the highest funding is 2Hire, which reached fundraising of 5 million euros.

The success the two UBAs brought to the two start-up ecosystems is mirrored in the exit strategies; indeed, during the last 2 years, two start-ups achieved an exit strategy in the CNS accelerator, while six start-ups accomplished an exit strategy in the LEL accelerator. However, no start-up of the two accelerators has yet managed to enter the stock market.

Qualitative data are interesting and useful in obtaining insights into how the two UBAs performed, although the ways to do that are also important. Indeed, in terms of the development of start-ups and the viability of these processes for the UBAs themselves, interesting answers emerged. The business model of the CNS accelerator is win-for-call or pay-for-support; thus, it does not become a member of the start-ups with which it works. If the start-up receives funding through calls, the support is free, while if the start-up fails to obtain funding, it must pay for the support services. Conversely, the business model of the LEL accelerator is equity for support. In any case, the accelerator becomes a stockholder of the start-up.

In both UBAs, the universities never fully enter the social structure except for start-ups that spun off from university departments.

For the CNS accelerator, the exit strategy is not a fundamental question; however, the contrary is true for the LEL accelerator due to its involvement in the cap table. As confirmation, the LEL accelerator has agreed with start-ups since the beginning that the main objective is to obtain a financial result within 5 years. Consequently, the LEL accelerator defines itself as a "pure financial operator" because a large part of the cap table is covered by a related investment fund. Conversely, start-ups accelerated by CNS seem less interested in achieving an exit strategy. These considerations are confirmed by the directors we interviewed, as reported in the following excerpts:

> . . . At CNS, we support the economic logic rather than the financial one; thus, we work to reconvert the territory and move from the so-called 'heavy industry' to a 'thinking industry' through innovation promoted by start-ups. . .
>
> (Manager of CNS).

> . . .LEL fundamentally acts as a financial operator. The main goal is to ensure that the investment fund that is part of our UBA may obtain an ROI as high as possible, making the start-ups we incubate as attractive as possible to be incorporated by large companies. . . .
>
> (Manager of LEL).

In the next subsections, the findings are presented with reference to the three perspectives—actors, geographical context, and resources—that emerged from the literature/main international start-up ecosystem:

6.1.1 Actors

First, UBAs support the entrepreneurs-to-be through core competence, that is, through managerial transfer thanks to a team of specialized mentors. Many mentors are recruited due to their university backgrounds, viz., many of them—as well as entrepreneurs—have previous experience in university teaching.

In this regard, the operating director of the CNS UBA stated the following:

> Our mentors are quite young but experienced. Therefore, they align so much with the way of thinking of potential start-uppers. We selected them based on their previous experience and on their specialization in certain industries.
>
> (Manager of CNS)

On the other hand, the Director of the Investment Fund at LEL UBA paid more attention to the background than to the age or specialization. Indeed, he said:

> Our team members are mostly financial specialists. They coordinate the rest of the team, but we leverage what we know we can do best, namely, increase as much as possible the profitability of our funds.
>
> (Manager of LEL)

The two UBAs behave differently because mentors are chosen based on different features. One more difference that emerged from the interviews is the role of the university community in mentoring the acceleration program. At CNS, the community is mainly instrumental for start-ups, while it is the opposite at LEL due to the financial-based goals.

One more element is worth being recalled from the interviews and with reference to actors, namely, the role of past start-uppers currently leading their firms. No involvement emerged in either of the two UBAs. Therefore, previous experience can simply be recalled by the UBA teams.

6.1.2 Geographical Context

Due to the features of the context of the UBAs, accelerators are supported, in turn, by universities, which often provide logistical solutions and laboratories. Similar considerations apply to the start-ups, as they benefit from the internal viability of the UBAs to develop in fertile ground.

A consideration stressing the topic above emerged from the interview with the Operating Director of the CNS:

> The set of local conditions made the difference in our development and in the growth of the start-up; the university provided something that can't be bought anywhere else, namely, the propensity to innovate. It is infused in the university community, in research groups, in the history of previous industrial relations, and so on. It truly made the difference for us and for start-ups.
>
> (Manager of CNS)

Similar considerations were also offered in the interviews at LEL; in any event, the context is seen as wider, as the participation of corporate investors, venture capitalists, and other firms acting in similar or connected industries expand the opportunities to meet start-uppers' needs and show them the right way to start their businesses.

Moreover, relations play a relevant role as, thanks to the accelerator, start-ups are inserted into larger circuits and ecosystems. Investor matching is also favored, expanding the nature of the start-up ecosystem from local to international; in some cases, partnering local start-ups with international firms was found to be useful. This consideration is particularly true at LEL, as the Director of the Investment Fund carefully described:

> We are not just a single entity as a consultancy firm; we are a hub, and we group multiple actors via a continuously growing set of relations to widen the opportunity a start-upper may find while setting everything to challenge the market. Investors and other firms acting as potential partners shape a unique combination to fund and launch a business.
> (Manager of LEL)

Finally, the context is also shaped differently from an equity-based perspective, as for the CNS UBAs, the university is an important part of the cap table (49%). Meanwhile, in LEL, the university has no share at all and takes care of mentoring, cobranding, and relations-building, also abroad.

6.1.3 Resources

Both UBAs report increasing the growth of the start-ups through several resources and their combination; indeed, core competence, technical and advanced resources, relationships, and prestige played fundamental roles. Overall, both CNS and LEL report promoting the growth of accelerated start-ups through these multiple resources.

Additionally (and one of the most relevant results), start-ups are offered a series of IT solutions for technological development, while logistical resources—such as operational headquarters—are offered. This is a feature strictly pertaining to a university-centered domain, as the Operating Director at CNS stated:

> There is a variety of knowledge one can't properly understand from the outside. Being one of the oldest universities with a multitude of departments led us to count on whatever we need. Thus, the main effort has been the organization of knowledge flows and their recombination in start-ups. As it concerns the recombination, the alignment between the learning orientation of start-uppers and the teaching approach of university members is crucial in favouring the success of a new business.
> (Manager of CNS)

Moreover, prestige is a distinctive feature of the two university-based accelerators. Many start-ups enter the stage as unknown entities, and the accelerator is committed to promoting them through public events, competition notices, and other means, such as university seminars. This consideration is tied to relationships as resources brought by the UBAs to the start-up ecosystem and to the start-ups looking for partners, investors, and external mentors, too.

Both accelerators usually contribute to start-up development through support that they define as *"making resources available: tangible, intangible, monetary"* (at CNS) and *"organizing matches with investors"* (at LEL); additionally, two relevant actions are to achieve fundraising and pave the way for open innovation. Nevertheless, two different approaches have been identified with regard to the process of switching from business idea to execution phase, as well as with reference to achieving an exit strategy. The LEL accelerator is not involved in switching to the execution; indeed, it chooses start-ups that already have at least one MVP (Minimum Viable Product). On the other hand, CNS supports the switch from business idea to execution phase; indeed, CNS accepts early-stage projects.

Finally, as an interplay between relations and prestige, several start-ups in the accelerators scaled the market and met market players thanks to the academic background of the accelerator; therefore, the counterpart elicited confidence due to the involvement of the university. This statement is supported by the response provided by the Director of the Investment Fund at LEL:

> . . .Being a UBA is an opportunity, both for start-ups and for the UBA itself; indeed, we are in an advantageous condition, since we don't need an introduction, as we are a UBA and this gives us credibility and inspires trust in start-uppers. They believe in the power of knowledge for continuous improvement and consider a university-based entity as the right partner. . . .
> (Manager of LEL)

6.2 *Main Evidence from the Interviews with Start-up Founders (Rome and Naples)*

The interviews with the founders of the main start-ups included in the ecosystems of Naples and Rome were, like the previous ones, conducted in narrative analysis mode following the three reference variables identified by the study: resources, actors, and geographical context.

The founders of the start-ups interviewed are managers of two start-ups: MegaRide and Foodys.

Among the main results of these interviews, one condition is immediately evident: that the start-ups established in ecosystems often significantly adapt to the configuration of the reference ecosystem and adapt and shape their own development goals.

These considerations are confirmed by the founders we interviewed, as reported in the following excerpts:

> . . .At MegaRide, we have never been interested in fundraising. We have had many very attractive proposals from venture capitalists which we have refused in favor of organic growth. Not even the debt capital market and bank loans have ever interested us. . . .
> (Manager of Megaride—Naples)

> . . .At OffLunch and Moovenda, we constantly aim to involve new investors in order to increase our premoney value . . . We propose a very convenient capital market for investors

who participate in investment rounds and who hope to be able to participate in the economic results as soon as possible. . . .
(Manager of Foodys—Rome)

Another important consideration should be made regarding the founders' perception of the role that the incubator, in which the two start-ups of the respective ecosystems of Rome and Naples are inserted, had in the development of their start-ups.

. . .at MegaRide we started doing open innovation: it all started immediately after my graduation when the Ferrari management called for a PhD aimed at the production of a software tool to improve the performance and grip of racing vehicles on the road . . . Among the various models, mine was chosen, the MegaRide one. . . Our incubator, Campania New Steel, has oriented us to business and put us in contact with a series of actors able to transfer important entrepreneurial skills in the field of business development. . . .
(Manager of Megaride—Naples)

. . .At Moovenda it all started with the Rome start-up week and from the first step of the incubation path in Luiss and labs where we received the first 80k mixed between money and services, financed by the first investment fund—L Ventures—which immediately entered into our cap table. . . .
(Manager of Foodys—Rome)

6.3 *Main Evidence from the Interviews with University Professors and Assistant Professors (Rome and Naples)*

In chapter "Start-up Ecosystems and Institutions: The Role of Universities and Academic Entrepreneurship", about local institutions as a means of supporting the birth and development of new and innovative businesses, we focused specifically on the role of universities.

As already described in the paragraph dedicated to the research methodology and the methodology process that we applied to this study, the professors of the main universities of Naples and Rome were also interviewed in narrative analysis mode.

In this section, we report the results of the interviews with professors and assistant professors engaged in academic entrepreneurship at the University Federico II of Naples, University La Sapienza of Rome, Luiss Guido Carli University of Rome, and John Cabot University of Rome.

The interviews were developed with some of our guidelines to highlight the specific commitments of the respective universities in supporting the start-ups of the reference ecosystem. The specific purpose was to detect emerging or already existing initiatives and the limits or prospects in the action of the universities in the start-up ecosystems of Naples and Rome, as well as any resources and tools that, according to the interviewees, are currently lacking and thereby preventing universities from performing at their best in supporting entrepreneurship.

The first consideration of this analysis of the academic staff involved in the topic of entrepreneurship is to highlight a countertrend with respect to the previous interviews with the founders of start-ups in the start-up ecosystems of Rome and Naples and the directors of the incubators of the same ecosystems of start-ups. The countertrend in this section concerns the fact that, unlike previous comparisons, this comparison shows a rather similar model of functioning of the role of the university. While the Rome start-ups pursue very different logics from those of Naples, just as the Neapolitan-certified incubator has a completely different model from that of Rome, the role of the universities of Rome and Naples, according to the information received from the interviewees, is very similar.

> ...The Federico II Spin-off Commission has decided not to develop spin-offs in which the university is part of the start-up cap tablel. We believe this is an advantage for those who found and carry on the academic spin-off start-up because the decision-making process would be much more cumbersome, having to convene the university spin-off commission every time. The spinoff status for start-ups is absolutely free and guarantees the founders many benefits....
>
> (Full Professor Federico II of Naples).

> ...There is a lot of commitment on the part of the universities of the Lazio region in supporting start-up companies but I think they are somewhat behind the international excellence. Only a few years ago, the attention of Italian universities had been directed to the world of entrepreneurship but in any case only in the didactic field. As part of the financial support, I would like to p,' in collaboration with LVenture Group, a private investment fund and naturally external to the univesity....
>
> (Assistant Professor University La Sapienza of Rome).

> Very often, the work of our departments is of a consultative nature and supports the development of ideas, but very rarely is the idea started, funded, and financed by the university ... We are more 'extrapreneur' than 'entrepreneur'....
>
> (Assistant Professor Federico II of Naples)

> ...The universities of the Lazio region have excellent university research centers and LUISS and John Cabot, among the private ones, those with greater attention to entrepreneurship from different points of view (Doc Tre, JCU Weekend of Start-ups). However, the latter struggle to build concrete relational bridges with the business world and above all with the world of venture capital....
>
> (Associate Professor University John Cabot of Rome).

Another important aspect that emerged from our interviews is the widespread awareness among professors and researchers that investing in entrepreneurship teaching is an advantageous choice: Students who benefit from learning for entrepreneurship develop knowledge of world skills and essential skills and attitudes, including creativity, initiative, tenacity, teamwork, risk awareness, and a sense of responsibility.

Italian universities, in particular, those of Rome and Naples, are doing a lot to become more "entrepreneurial and start-up oriented" despite the great limits that differentiate us from the entrepreneurial ecosystems of excellence.

> ...I notice both from the point of view of numbers and performance an imbalance between the spin-offs born from the various departments of Federico II. There are very dynamic departments and others that have never made a spin-off ....
>
> (Full professor Federico II of NAples)

> ...There are three issues to accelerate the process of diffusion of academic entrepreneurship. The first is a question of timing, that is, the earlier, the better. I have had experience with master's-degree, three-year-degree. The second is a question of intensity. A course, an event, or a book is not enough; it is important to expose young people in many ways to the concept of entrepreneurship. The third is the idea of creating a system: We win if we are placed in a 'fertile' context, in which the ecosystem truly works....
> (Associate professor of University John Cabot of Rome)

From what emerged from the interviews, it is evident that the Italian entrepreneurial academic culture has not yet spread sufficiently, especially compared to American university contexts. As we have pointed out, one of the main obstacles is the lower presence of capital and investment funds connected to Italian universities.

On the other hand, it must be said that the commitment of the universities of Rome and Naples with regard to entrepreneurial education is considerable (and the results of the interviews that follow testify to this) (Carayannis et al., 2003; Clarke et al., 2020)—namely, the set of teachings with the intent of equipping students with the knowledge, skills, and motivation to encourage entrepreneurial success in a variety of contexts. Entrepreneurship education is about content, methods, and activities in support of the creation and development of knowledge, skills, and experiences that make it desirable and possible for students to start and participate in the creation processes of entrepreneurial value.

Experts—both professors and professionals—have finally realized that many university students have the intention of starting a new business. Intervention through training courses from the early years of university is essential to ensuring that students develop adequate skills and attitudes.

The results of the interviews show that the programs of the universities of Rome are more structured than those of Naples, even if in the latter the ground is being prepared for a disciplinary extension. As emerges from the interviews, the activities in the "Entrepreneurship Education" direction of Federico II, despite being connected to important networks, including international ones, aim at a structural strengthening that will make it possible to obtain interesting organizational inputs also through internal initiatives.

6.4 *Evidence from the Interviews with Representatives of Silicon Valley*

Below are the contents of the interviews made with various exponents of the Silicon Valley start-up ecosystem, including scholars and communicators of the start-up topic, serial founders of start-ups, and important investors. The interviews reported are those of:

- *Jim Spohrer,* Investor and Serial Manager; Founding Member of the International Society of Service Innovation Professionals. (Interview done directly by the

author, as well as the previous ones with directors of accelerators, start-up founders, and university professors).
- *Steve Blank* (Results taken from the interviews made by the journalists Eleonora Chioda and Tiziana Tripepi and available on their work, 2019).
- Joseph Huang, CEO of the Stanford University incubator: StartX (Results taken from the interviews made by the journalists Eleonora Chioda and Tiziana Tripepi and available in their work, 2019).

The goal of investigating and describing the Silicon Valley start-up ecosystem is based on the desire to perform a benchmarking analysis for our Italian ecosystem (split in two: Rome and Naples) using Silicon Valley as a reference. Thanks to the results of the interview with the aforementioned representatives, supplemented by various reports and rewriting contributions available online, we describe all the actors who, over the years, have contributed to increasing the mechanism for creating innovation and businesses. The constituent elements of this success, according to the contributions and interview results, are as follows.

We have divided the results into three identified Silicon Valley elements of success. The three strengths of Silicon Valley are technology, culture, and capital (Berlin, 2017).

6.4.1 Technology

Silicon Valley is the first zone in the world to use and access several new technologies, such as robotics, artificial intelligence, and the Internet of Things.

Through the contributions of various scholars, it is understandable to learn that in Silicon Valley, there are no simple professional figures who are experts in technological development, but there are profiles who, in addition to possessing soft skills, also have "a little something more." In Silicon Valley, there is a large presence of subjects defined by the literature as "Technopreneur" (Harlanu & Nugroho, 2015; Siregar et al., 2020). "A technopreneur means an entrepreneur who involves and deals with technology in their business. A technopreneur believes that technology would increase efficiency, productivity, product quality, broaden the market and helps to market the developed product widely" (Harlanu & Nugroho, 2015, p, 148). In addition to computer skills, these subjects have intangible and distinctive qualities and abilities such as intuition, ability, flair, and perseverance.

These concepts clearly emerge from the selected interviews:

> . . . analysing the territory of Silicon Valley well allows you to immediately understand that you need to focus on completely cutting-edge technologies and not on already consolidated ones such as "apps and social networks. A lot of innovation is happening by applying new technologies in the field of health and life science: medical diagnostics, medical devices, digital health. . . .
>
> (Steve Blank)

> …In 2000, I worked in the technology department of IBM, and through venture capital, we were already investing in many start-ups. Many of these failed but we were interested in hiring and having access to their CTO to expand our technologies….
> (Jim Spohrer)

> …in Silicon Valley, there are many examples of open innovation between start-ups and large companies: collaboration on open-source data and AI—for example, Horovod started at Uber/start-up and many big companies contribute to the Horovod project—so start-ups and big companies collaborate in open source and open innovation frequently around AI, since it is so hard, and thus far from being solved….
> (Jim Spohrer)

6.4.2 Culture

During the following book, we have had the opportunity to address how closely the concept of entrepreneurial culture is connected to that of education and training; in fact, we have referred to the concept of entrepreneurial education (Pittaway & Cope, 2007; Wilson, 2008; Consolini et al., 2013; Antonaci et al., 2014; Vanevenhoven, 2013).

Over the years, Silicon Valley has undergone highly qualified immigration (Saxenian, 2000). Many immigrants from Canada, Europe, and Asia were already profiles with medium-high skills who arrived to perfect their curriculum above all through the training offered by Stanford. Hundreds of Silicon Valley companies founded by immigrants are now worth hundreds of millions. Just think of the story of Steve Jobs who founded Apple in a garage in Cupertino. Jobs' mother was Swiss, and his father was Syrian. The adoptive parents promised the natural ones that Jobs would go to an excellent university in California. Job did not graduate, but through the University of Berkeley, he met his electrical engineer partner Steve Wozniak (Blumenthal, 2012).

The influence that, directly or indirectly, the universities of Silicon Valley have on aspiring entrepreneurs is evident from the content of the answers to the interview reported by Joseph Huang, CEO of the Stanford University incubator, and from the interview that the author did directly to opinion leader Jim Spohrer.

> …StartX is not a profit accelerator, where experts take care of training start-ups and in exchange obtain company shares. Nor is it a training program that lasts for weeks. StartX is a community of serial entrepreneurs, start-up founders, students, researchers and professors from the University of Stanford….
> (Joseph Huang)

> … in Italy you could create an environment similar to this to obtain a successful start-up ecosystem. Stimulate the sharing of ideas between industry, universities, researchers, professors and professionals. A mixed group can do much more than we can do individually….
> (Joseph Huang)

As we have seen, Stanford (followed by Berkeley) performed the function of the anchor tenant, attracting large companies for research and development and government funds to Silicon Valley. From universities, the most "disruptive" innovations were born, and thanks to entrepreneurial education and the work of professors and researchers, these innovations have been translated into globally successful companies. In summary, universities in Silicon Valley have the role of educating students from both technical and entrepreneurial points of view, attracting the largest companies in the world for research and development, managing to concentrate laboratories and a lot of human capital specialized in one place, and being able to make technology transfer with research done in collaboration with the state.

In the United States, the university is connected to the world of venture capital, while in Italy, it does not work the same way. Even in the start-up ecosystem of Rome, where compared to that of Naples, there are certainly more investment funds and venture capital, there is no connection to the venture capital market within the university.

> .... In Silicon Valley but also in other U.S. start-up ecosystems, universities are often equipped with financial tools to invest in start-ups and to finance academic spinoffs....
> (J. Spohrer)

> ... Universities provide two other important things to start-up ecosystems, namely, 'human capital' and 'research results' applicable to business... Start-ups consider universities to be truly important for the provision of human capital and soft skills....
> (J. Spohrer)

> ...Stanford and Berkeley are the most influential universities in the Californian start-up ecosystem mainly in the Information Technology sector ....
> (Jim Spohrer)

6.4.3 Capital

Since the first start-ups, there has always been the investor component, which, in addition to providing large sums of money, provides support for management to temporally compress and thus accelerate the growth process. In Silicon Valley, the start-up investor has become a real professional role, with an organizational model imitated all over the world.

According to the results of the interviews, two decisive cultural factors immediately emerged. The first is that for the entrepreneurial culture of Silicon Valley, failure is not seen in a negative sense but, instead, as a valid starting point. The second is that investments by venture capitalists are not made solely to participate in future economic results but also occur because some players, through the investment, are interested in becoming part of a new reality from which to capture new competence and soft skills.

> The secret of Silicon Valley is a high concentration of money and crazy people.
> (Steve Blank)

> ...at IBM, we were also interested in the profile of the customers of the start-ups we purchased to see if they were the same as ours or if they differed... We aimed more at

> acquiring resources, skills, and information and not so much at the economic value of start-ups...
> (J. Spohrer)

> ...The secret of start-up fundraising is relationships. It is rare for a major venture capitalist to meet someone he has not known in other circumstances or who has been introduced to him. Venture capital is a business based on networks and trust; in fact, it is called—introduction business...
> (Steve Blank).

We have described Silicon Valley as the land of innovation and creativity and as a business where anything is possible. However, the coronavirus pandemic has reopened the discussion on a very well-known issue lately among those involved in the technology industry in the United States: the future of Silicon Valley and, for the most pessimistic, its crisis. The Economist coined the term "techlash" the backlash, referring to the media opinion toward big tech that until very recently had never been questioned.

In fact, some data are cause for concern. For example, there is a high cost of living (1.2 million dollars average price of a house, the average in the United States is 221,000 dollars). Many workers find it difficult to rent an economically viable home. In addition, there is a traffic problem in the city with an average of 1 h a day. Gender equality also reports a negative figure, i.e., while the average income of the population is 140,000 dollars, women earn 33% less (Silicon Valley Index, 2020).

With respect to this scenario, start-up experts and scholars still do not go too far. Steve Blank asserts: "if someone wants to turn dreams into reality he must absolutely stop in Silicon Valley."

7 Conclusion

This book responded to the demand for further research into the elements mentioned in this work that serves as a suggestion for an international interpretive model of start-up ecosystems. Depending on the geographical and sociocultural situations, each one might acquire varying degrees of prominence and impact. With the help of literature and start-up ecosystem insights, we were able to create a study framework based on players, geographic context, and resources.

This proposal for an interpretative model starts from the description of the main components that constitute and form the start-up ecosystem: the start-up companies integrated into entrepreneurial ecosystems; incubators accelerators that provide support to start-up companies; institutions, and in particular the role of universities; and accessibility to new technologies.

Start-up companies are changing their characteristics over the years and follow the changes of the digital revolution. The geographical contexts in which they are inserted determine their ability to access fundamental resources. Business incubators and accelerators are a determining factor in the proliferation of start-ups within ecosystems. Business incubators and accelerators have very different models at an international level but the purpose of supporting the creation and development of start-ups unites them all. The role of universities as the main actor in the entrepreneurial momentum of a territory, albeit through different methods and degrees, is also spreading in Italy but only partially and very slowly assuming the characteristics of the United States. Regardless of the models of the organizations that support start-ups (incubators, accelerators, universities, etc.) all of these aim to make new technologies increasingly accessible to the service of start-up companies that want to aim for scalability of the market in which they are inserted. The initial model is enriched by three fundamental variables identified during the study: actors, resources, and geographical contexts, which are useful for explore and to explode the components initially identified.

This book proposes some implications, both theoretical and practical, of the research that the author has developed before and after his PhD student period. Three major consequences are identified among the theoretical ramifications. The first is methodological in character and specifically relates to the suggestion of a model for interpreting ecosystem start-ups. The framework specifies five important components, including universities, incubators, accelerators, start-ups, and access to technology that are investigated using the three variables indicated by the international literature. Infusing reports with spatial settings-resources-actors. An integration of the prior observations is a different type of inference. The approach previously discussed could be helpful for future study since academics and professors are now aware that the subject of start-ups has grown so pervasive that it no longer simply affects individuals who aspire to be entrepreneurs. The introductions' evolution of the phenomenon-related facts speak for themselves. This makes it desirable that future research on the subject of start-up ecosystems include a multi-faceted approach. It would be preferable to take a different approach from one that looks for working mechanisms to explain the proliferation of start-ups and instead concentrates on describing how actors, resources, and processes adapt to and shape themselves in response to various geographical, sociocultural, and historical contexts. In this approach, identification and identification become "deeper," no longer post-phenomenological, and as a result, encompass not only ways of improvement but also the origins of Start-up Ecosystems, which have a more or less favorable effect on future developments.

Regarding the practical implications, it should be noted that research, reports from around the world, and interviews conducted in various contexts and at various levels demonstrate how financial support (hence, Venture Capital, private funds, Business Angles) and "formative" support in terms of knowledge transfer, skills development, and skills influence the emergence and growth of new innovative companies. The investigation of this work in particular enables us to claim that the existence of venture capital in ecosystems is unquestionably a more common condition in American geographic contexts than in European geographic contexts. Additionally, it is obvious that the availability of Venture Capital financial instruments has a direct impact on the near-term performance of start-up businesses, shortening the time required to move from the MVP (Multiple Viable Product) phase to the Early Stage and Execution phases of the start-ups established in their internal. On the other hand, support services, mentoring, skills transfer by incubators, accelerators and universities ("European model"), on the contrary, have more long-term implications such as the diffusion of entrepreneurial culture in ecosystems, an easier access to higher entrepreneurial training and collaboration between public and private institutions and new innovative companies.

Finally, based on the findings, it can be assumed that "failure as a good occurrence" is not a culture in the Italian and European ecosystems. But in the States, being aware of one's errors is frequently the cornerstone of success. Failure and invention are symbiotic partners. Additionally, it should be mentioned that the common adage "9 out of 10 start-ups fail" lacks empirical support, as the interviews with managers, founders, incubator directors, and entrepreneurship researchers (although with a small sample) clearly demonstrate. The problem facing today's Italian start-ups is not short-term failure, but rather what is known as "dwarfism": they endure for a long time without ever being able to accomplish crucial development milestones like significant exits or stock market listings. Allowing a founders' and shareholders' return on investment is more challenging for Italian start-ups.

Acknowledgments The book is the result of a collaborative effort undertaken over time and from multiple point of view.

It is appropriate and indispensable to thank and mention a series of scholars and professionals essential for the preparation of this book.

My current mentor and guide of the scientific project at the basis of my researcher contract with the Federico II University of Naples professor Francesco Bifulco. must be thanked.

I must also thank the coordinator of my PhD and supervisor of my doctoral thesis from which this book was inspired, Professor Cristina Mele.

My thanks also go to Professor Tiziana Russo Spena and Professor Marco Tregua who supported me in drafting this manuscript.

I thank the directors of business incubators and accelerators, the founders of start-up companies and the professors of Italian universities for the precious interviews they gave me.

References

Adams, S. B. (2018). A diversified portfolio: Resources fueling Silicon Valley before venture capital. In *Business history conference. Business and economic history on-line: Papers presented at the BHC annual meeting* (Vol. 16, pp. 1–14). Business History Conference.

Antonaci, A., Bellotti, F., Berta, R., Dagnino, F. M., De Gloria, A., Lavagnino, E., & Ott, M. (2014). Educazione all'imprenditorialità: spunti di riflessione. *Italian Journal of Educational Technology, 22*(2), 68–73.

Audretsch, D. B., & Belitski, M. (2017). Entrepreneurial ecosystems in cities: Establishing the framework conditions. *The Journal of Technology Transfer, 42*, 1030–1051.

Baloutsos, S., Karagiannaki, A., & Mourtos, I. (2020). Business Model Generation for Industry 4.0: A "Lean Startup" approach. *The International Technology Management Review, 9*(1), 34–45.

Bania, N., Eberts, R. W., & Fogarty, M. S. (1993). Universities and the start-up of new companies: Can we generalize from route 128 and Silicon Valley? *The Review of Economics and Statistics, 75*, 761–766.

Berger, E. S., & Kuckertz, A. (2016). Female entrepreneurship in startup ecosystems worldwide. *Journal of Business Research, 69*(11), 5163–5168.

Berlin, L. (2017). *Troublemakers: Silicon Valley's coming of age*. Simon and Schuster.

Bernhofer, L., & Han, Z. (2014). Contextual factors and their effects on future entrepreneurs in China: A comparative study of entrepreneurial intentions. *International Journal of Technology Management, 65*(1–4), 125–150.

Bliemel, M., & Flores, R. G. (2015). Defining and differentiating accelerators: Insights from the Australian context. In *Academy of management proceedings* (Vol. 2015, No. 1, p. 14151). Briarcliff Manor, NY 10510: Academy of Management.

Blumenthal, K. (2012). *Steve jobs the man who thought different*. Imprints of Macmillan.

Boje, D. M. (1991). Consulting and change in the storytelling organisation. *Journal of Organizational Change Management, 4*(3), 7–17.

Breznitz, S. M., & Zhang, Q. (2019). Fostering the growth of student start-ups from university accelerators: An entrepreneurial ecosystem perspective. *Industrial and Corporate Change, 28* (4), 855–873.

Buchnik, T., Gilad, V., & Maital, S. (2018). Universities' influence on student decisions to become entrepreneurs: Theory and evidence. *Journal of Entrepreneurship Education, 21*(3), 1–19.

Carayannis, E. G., Evans, D., & Hanson, M. (2003). A cross-cultural learning strategy for entrepreneurship education: Outline of key concepts and lessons learned from a comparative study of entrepreneurship students in France and the US. *Technovation, 23*(9), 757–771.

Chioda E.; Tripepi T., (2019) Silicon Valley, cosa imparare dalla terra dell'innovazione per farcela in Italia,. Hoepli.

Clarke, D., Romano, J. P., & Wolf, M. (2020). The Romano–Wolf multiple-hypothesis correction in Stata. *The Stata Journal, 20*(4), 812–843.

Cohen. (2006). What do accelerators do? Insights from incubators and angels. *Innovations: Technology, Governance, Globalization, 8*.

Cohen, S., Fehder, D. C., Hochberg, Y. V., & Murray, F. (2019). The design of startup accelerators. *Research Policy, 48*(7), 1781–1797.

Consolini, M., Di Saverio, M., Loasses, C., & Richini, P. (2013). Indicazioni per la programm zione e la realizzazione di iniziative per l'educazione all'imprenditorialità.

Cukier, D., & Kon, F. (2018). A maturity model for software startup ecosystems. *Journal of Innovation and Entrepreneurship, 7*(1), 1–32.

Cukier, D., Kon, F., & Lyons, T. S. (2016, June). Software startup ecosystems evolution: The New York City case study. In *2016 International Conference on Engineering, Technology and Innovation/IEEE International Technology Management Conference (ICE/ITMC)* (pp. 1–8). IEEE.

Dempwolf, C. S., Auer, J., & D'ippolito, M. (2014). Innovation accelerators: Defining characteristics among startup assistance organizations. *Small Business Administration, 10*, 1–44.

Etzkowitz, H. (2013). Anatomy of the entrepreneurial university. *Social Science Information, 52*(3), 486–511.

Etzkowitz, H. (2022). Entrepreneurial university icon: Stanford and Silicon Valley as innovation and natural ecosystem. *Industry and Higher Education, 36*(4), 361–380.

Etzkowitz, H., & Zhou, C. (2017). *The triple helix: University–industry–government innovation and entrepreneurship*. Routledge.

Fraiberg, S. (2017). Start-up nation: Studying transnational entrepreneurial practices in Israel's start-up ecosystem. *Journal of Business and Technical Communication, 31*(3), 350–388.

Franco-Leal, N., Camelo-Ordaz, C., Fernandez-Alles, M., & Sousa-Ginel, E. (2019). The entrepreneurial ecosystem: Actors and performance in different stages of evolution of academic spinoffs. *Entrepreneurship Research Journal, 10*(2), 20180228.

Genome. (2022). Official Website of Report Genome. www.startupgenome.com

Goyal, S., Sergi, B. S., & Jaiswal, M. P. (2016). Understanding the challenges and strategic actions of social entrepreneurship at base of the pyramid. *Management Decision*.

Greco, F., & Tregua, M. (2022). It gives you wheels: The university-based accelerators in start-up ecosystems. *International Journal of Entrepreneurship and Small Business, 45*(2), 235–257.

Harlanu, M., & Nugroho, A. (2015). The importance of technopreneurship management model for vocational school. In *3rd UPI international conference on technical and vocational education and training* (pp. 147–150). Atlantis Press, part of Springer Nature.

Hemmert, M., Cross, A. R., Cheng, Y., Kim, J. J., Kohlbacher, F., Kotosaka, M., et al. (2019). The distinctiveness and diversity of entrepreneurial ecosystems in China, Japan, and South Korea: An exploratory analysis. *Asian Business & Management, 18*, 211–247.

Hernández, C., & González, D. (2016). Study of the start-up ecosystem in Lima, Peru: Collective case study. *Latin American Business Review, 17*(2), 115–137.

Infocamere. (2021). Official site of the company of the Italian trade office for digital innovation. www.infocamere.it

Joshi, K., & Satyanarayana, K. (2014). What ecosystem factors impact the growth of high-tech start-ups in India? *Asian Journal of Innovation and Policy, 3*(2), 216–244.

Kanbach, D. K., & Stubner, S. (2016). Corporate accelerators as recent form of startup engagement: The what, the why, and the how. *Journal of Applied Business Research (JABR), 32*(6), 1761–1776.

Kenney, M. (2000). *Understanding Silicon Valley: The anatomy of an entrepreneurial region*. Stanford University Press.

Krajcik, V., & Formanek, I. (2015). Regional startup ecosystem. *European Business & Management, 1*(2), 14–18.

Laužikas, M., & Dailydaitė, S. (2015). Impacts of social capital on transformation from efficiency to innovation-driven business. *Journal of Business Economics and Management, 16*(1), 37–51.

Leslie, S. W., & Kargon, R. H. (1996). Selling Silicon Valley: Frederick Terman's model for regional advantage. *Business History Review, 70*(4), 435–472.

Lojek, B. (2007). Shockley semiconductor laboratories. *History of Semiconductor Engineering*, 67–101.

Malecki, E. J. (2018). Entrepreneurship and entrepreneurial ecosystems. *Geography Compass, 12* (3), e12359.

Mansoori, Y., Karlsson, T., & Lundqvist, M. (2019). The influence of the lean startup methodology on entrepreneur-coach relationships in the context of a startup accelerator. *Technovation, 84*, 37–47.

Miles, M. P., & Morrison, M. (2020). An effectual leadership perspective for developing rural entrepreneurial ecosystems. *Small Business Economics, 54*, 933–949.

MISE. (2021). Official website of the Italian economic-political-financial newspaper. Sole 24 Ore. www.sole24ore.it

Petretto L. (2007) Imprenditore ed Università nello start up di impresa, ruoli e relazioni critiche. Firenze University Press.

Pittaway, L., & Cope, J. (2007). Entrepreneurship education: A systematic review of the ev dence. *International Small Business Journal, 25*(5), 479–510.

Rome Start-up Association. (2021). Official site of the startup association of Rome. www.romastartup.it

Saxenian, A. (2000). Silicon Valley's new immigrant entrepreneurs.

Sipola, S., Puhakka, V., & Mainela, T. (2016). A start-up ecosystem as a structure and context for high growth. In *Global entrepreneurship: Past, present & future*. Emerald Group Publishing Limited.

Siregar, D., Purnomo, A., Mastuti, R., Napitupulu, D., Sadalia, I., Sutiksno, D. U., et al. (2020). *Technopreneurship: Strategi dan Inovasi*. Yayasan Kita Menulis.

Sole24Ore. (2019). Official website of the Italian economic-political-financial newspaper. Sole 24 Ore. www.sole24ore.it

Stayton, J., & Mangematin, V. (2019). Seed accelerators and the speed of new venture creation. *The Journal of Technology Transfer, 44*, 1163–1187.

Steiber, A., Alänge, S., Steiber, A., & Alänge, S. (2016). *The silicon valley model* (pp. 143–155). Springer International Publishing.

Tripathi, N., Seppänen, P., Boominathan, G., Oivo, M., & Liukkunen, K. (2019). Insights into startup ecosystems through exploration of multi-vocal literature. *Information and Software Technology, 105*, 56–77.

Vanevenhoven, J. (2013). Advances and challenges in entrepreneurship education. *Journal of Small Business Management, 51*(3), 466–470.

Ventura, R., Quero, M. J., & Diaz-Mendez, M. (2020). The role of institutions in achieving radical innovation. *Marketing Intelligence & Planning, 38*(3), 310–324.

Wilson, K. E. (2008). Entrepreneurship education in Europe. In *Entrepreneurship and higher education*.

The manufacturer's authorised representative in the EU is Springer Nature Customer Service Centre GmbH, Europaplatz 3, 69115 Heidelberg, Germany. If you have any concerns regarding our products, please contact ProductSafety@springernature.com

Printed and bound by CPI Group (UK) Ltd, Croydon, CR0 4YY
01/10/2026
02225883-0002